HIGH P

CLAUDIA SHEAR

AND HER "HILARIOUS"* TOUR DE RÉSUMÉ

BLOWN SIDEWAYS THROUGH LIFE

"RAUNCHY, FUNNY, DELICIOUSLY
REVENGEFUL."—*Cosmopolitan*

"Claudia Shear reminds us that when you gotta
work, do it on your own terms, with your own
style."—*Newsweek*

"HILARIOUS . . . [Claudia Shear] wittily and defi-
antly recounts her stunted stints as waiter, reception-
ist, nude model, proofreader, even con man's secretary. Not only will Shear inspire in you admiration
for all m
ve

"CLAUD
she ha
diminish
fessed b
tobiogra
is peppe
ries ab
page, Sh
nered c

Ple

BLOWN
SIDEWAYS
Through
LIFE

Claudia Shear

Delta
Trade Paperbacks

A Delta Book
Published by
Dell Publishing
a division of
Bantam Doubleday Dell Publishing Group, Inc
1540 Broadway
New York, New York 10036

The trademark Delta® is registered in the U.S. Patent and Trademark Office and in other countries.

ISBN: 0-385-31315-2

Reprinted by arrangement with The Dial Press

Manufactured in the United States of America
Published simultaneously in Canada

BVG 01

To my mother, my sister, and my brother-in-law, who have never been fired

I would like to thank:

Christopher Ashley, whose quality of mind and generosity of spirit were part of this work from the very beginning

James Nicola, because it was his idea for me to write in the first place

Everyone at the New York Theatre Workshop, who encouraged me throughout the entire production

Nina Ryan, who was my great friend long before she was my great literary agent

Susan Kamil, for being my editor with such patience, wisdom, and enthusiasm

And most of all, I would like to thank anyone who ever had to work with me.

CONTENTS

Prologue

It's three o'clock and I'm sitting on a bench putting on a pair of cop shoes. . . .

It's ten-thirty in the morning and I'm standing in a corner of a dirty basement tying on a big white apron. . . .

It's every Wednesday at eleven A.M. and I'm pulling on thick janitor's gloves and picking up a bucket. . . .

It's four-fifteen in the morning and I'm trying to take a nap in a bathroom on Wall Street by balancing my head on the toilet-paper roll. . . .

It's five o'clock and I sharpen my pencils. . . .

I sharpen my knife. . . .

I fasten on a phone headset. . . .

I totally undress. . . .

I put on lipstick. . . .

I tie a bow tie. . . .

I put on Mardi Gras beads. . . .

I button up a uniform shirt. . . .

A cook's jacket. . . .

My employee smock. . . .

My tasteful blazer. . . .

My long black skirt. . . .

My Pez dispenser. ("Okay," they tell me, "we want to give a funky, friendly feeling here, so all the hostesses have to give out Pez.")

And then I carry up cases of beer, tubs of chicken, stacks of documents, flats of eggs, trays of lipsticks. I set up the computer, the desk, the roux, the stock. I read the documents, chop the onions, wash the walls, wash the dishes, wash the pots, pour the drinks, answer the phone, answer the phone, answer the phone.

"Good afternoon, Battle, Fowler, Jaffin and Kheel . . ."

"Good morning, Shakespeare Festival . . ."

"Buona sera, Le Madri . . ."

"Hiii. We have five very pretty girls. Two brunettes, a redhead, and two very busty blondes. It's ninety-five for the hour, seventy-five for the half hour. That includes French and straight, coming twice in the hour, once in the half hour. . . ."

"NYU Medical Center Patient Information, what room, please?"

And they tell me, "Chill on the conversation."

"Don't stand over there!"

"Be nice to the customers!"

"Put your book away! No reading allowed!"

"Don't sit down."

"Here's a club in case they come to rob the restaurant late at night when I'm not here."

"Watch your mouth!"

"No eating!"

"Don't detach yourself from the console without permission."

"Remember to always give your name."

"Never give your name!"

And then, later, I hear, "Uh, there's been complaints about your attitude."

"You were heard whistling in the elevator. . . ."

". . . singing in the dining room. . . ."

"You talk too much. . . ."

"Your laugh is too loud. . . ."

"You have to do what we tell you to do. No arguments!"

"You spend too much time on the phone."

"Maybe you should drink less coffee—you won't have to go to the bathroom so much."

"The floor runs better when it's all men."

"No standing around! Look busy!"

"The girls wear leotards because that is what our customers like."

And my personal favorite: "I don't have to give you a reason. It's *my* restaurant!"

And finally:

"Listen, we're going to have to let you go. . . ."

"Um, after this week we won't need you."

"Oh, this is your last shift."

"Uh, there's going to be some changes in the schedule. . . ."

"Well, it's my way or the highway."

"You're fired!"

"Get out and don't come back!"

And every time I just say, "All right, all right, all right."

But sometimes, sometimes I say, "FUCK YOU!"

BLOWN SIDEWAYS

Most people seem to live in character. They have a beginning, a middle, and an end. They have a class, they have a place, they know what is becoming in them and what is due to them. But there is also another kind of life. One gets hit by some unusual transverse force, one is jerked out of one's stratum, and one lives crosswise for the rest of the time.

That's me. Blown sideways through life.

I'm from Brooklyn, that's where I'm from, dancing the rhumba with my mom to "Green Eyes." Enthralled by the incredible glamour of the bad kid, I tried to keep up, running from cop cars with the friends I carefully chose—girls like Janine Morelli, who was mean and punched me like a boy—or hanging out in a park on Avenue P.

Oh, God, did I want "in." In with Kathleen and Debby and Ronnie, skinny girls with fat asses in shiny fabrics who bit their nails and painted them anyway.

They all had younger brothers and sisters who they were supposed to watch while their mothers went shopping or went to the track dressed in their daughters' clothing. Vicious little kids with rotting baby teeth who would wait on freezing corners while their big sisters pushed up against cars with their boyfriends. (The girls faked the sex and heat, while the boys really suffered.)

We were tough. We "hung out." Not like other girls who didn't know about feeling-up and tongue-kissing. We broke bottles and made out in alleyways and hid our cigarettes in bushes near our houses only to retrieve them the next day, crushing leaves between our fingers to mask the smell of smoke.

I was a prime target. God knows how they knew I was different. At first guys would ask me out. I smoked and cursed and fought and stuffed my bra with tissues. But the part of me that still believed in Narnia and cried for Black Beauty must have somehow given me away.

"Yo, Claudia! I wanna break up with you!" (To regain status in the group they'd break up with me in front of everyone.)

"Great!" I would spit. "I thought you'd never fucking ask!"

Then I would walk home, crying to the sky. A sick twist, loving those who hate you.

One "P-Park" summer I left behind my tank tops

6

and bad attitude. Where I was going they weren't needed. My mom's friend's sister was married to a man named Harry, who was a dairy farmer in upstate New York. I went to work for him, to join his six daughters, who worked on the farm like ten men.

Harry was lanky and skinny. The back of his neck was like leather. He would make jokes and laugh to himself with his eyes shut and his mouth open. He was the kindest man in the world, but I think he was a terrible farmer. The cows were mangy and the barns were messy and if news of a health inspection reached us we would have to clean frantically all night long.

The farm was falling apart, yet Harry bought himself an enclosed tractor with air-conditioning and a radio. He'd haul me up and let me ride with him as he wailed along with the country music on the radio. Standing behind him I would examine him, scrutinize this foreign creature, this someone else's daddy who was so flawed and funny and always there.

My own father left right after I was born. He was a fire chief. When he came to visit he'd pull up in full uniform in a huge red car driven by a chauffeur named Jack. My father's nickname was "Handsome Bud" and he smelled of pipes and shaving cream. He always wore a white silk scarf. Every Sunday in church I prayed, "Let Mommy and Daddy get back together," until the words ceased to have any meaning and became an automatic gibber I said without thinking, without hope.

Back in my basement in Brooklyn I read books that ranged from *The Divine Comedy* to Book-of-the-Month Club selections of the late 1950s. I read anything I could get my hands on. A misfit in Flatbush, I wanted out so badly, I wanted to fit in so much: late at night in "P-Park," breaking windows, dry-humping in doorways, staggering home, vomiting cheap wine into the gutter. Then, the next day, sullen in my filthy school-uniform blouse, called before the principal again, waiting for my mother to arrive, flawlessly chic, bone thin, and smelling of Secret of Venus.

My mother drove a white sports car. She smoked Pall Mall cigarettes and drank black coffee. Long necked, in sleeveless sheaths of slinky knits that she wore with a careless scattering of tiny antique pins, my mother had real style. Her hair was a smooth bubble of ash-blond held in place by Just Wonderful! hairspray and nightly wrappings of toilet paper. She wore eyeliner, lipstick, and fluttery fake eyelashes. Her favorite hat was a stiff, domed turban of iridescent bird feathers. I couldn't wait to grow up and wear a hat like that.

My mother worked for a cosmetics company. She spent her days driving between Bonwit's and Bergdorf's and B. Altman's, while my sister and I spent our days at school. She would pull into the driveway late at night, and sometimes, as a special treat, we would wait up, dish towels draped over our arms, fake menus in our hands, and play waiters in our flowery pj's. We were nine years old, but we knew how to be hostesses. She had already taught us how to clean crystal (vinegar and newspaper), to set a table for a buffet (fan the silver cutlery in careful arcs), to iron linen (while damp, apply starch and leave in the refrigerator until you are ready to iron), which kind of pasta goes with which sauce (long, thin pasta for fish sauce, thick macaronis for meat-based), how to introduce ourselves, how to pass hors d'oeuvres, to embroider, crochet, sew, and why the lace doilies on chair backs are called "antimacassars" (in the "olden days" men used Macassar oil as a hair pomade and doilies were used to protect the furniture).

One day my mother took a work route that passed our school. She pulled up, then walked over to the chain link fence that surrounded the yard where we were playing and smiled a big, lit-up, movie-star smile. None of the other mothers looked like my mom. None of them was divorced. None of them had a different last name than their kids. But most definitely none of them smiled the way she did.

When she drove away all the other kids said, "Hey! How come your mother wears so much makeup, huh? How come?"

"Because . . . !" I screamed back at them, proud, humiliated, and angry, ". . . because she *has* to!"

Other girls didn't get into trouble the way I did. I was defiant. I'd learned this lying blank-faced and un-flinching after a year of bruises from living with my father and his new wife. I was captured by Indians that year. I don't remember the story, but I think it was in a book called *Calico Captive*. The young hero-ine is rescued and given a hot bath. The hottest bath ever. Almost painful. She is bathed with scented soap and washed clean. Living there, in my father's house, my world slipped on its axis. The universe was askew. I wasn't really eight anymore. The day you know dan-ger and fear, and know that you are alone, is the day you grow, if not up, then old.

But inside my head there was romance: running through the Highlands with Alan Breck, Crusoe on a desert island, atop a magic mountain, astride a horse with wings. I wanted adventure. A cottage in the woods with the enchanted sword. The search for the Holy Grail. The trials of the hero. All for the quest! Inside my head I was suffering and striving in great feats of strength and ennobling tests of character. This was the plan of my life, the concept perfectly framed.

But what actually was my life?

At last count I've had sixty-five jobs, and some of them of unusually short duration, the briefest being at a restaurant called Bar Lui: Got hired. Went to work.

Drank an iced coffee. Made a few phone calls. After about ten minutes the manager interrupted me.

"Um, we have very specific policies regarding personal calls. . . ."

"Oh, *please*," I muttered, "you must be fucking kidding."

So I got my coat, got my keys, my token, my ticket, my passport, my cash card, and I hit the road, Jack. Out the door on a subway, a train, a plane, a bus. Walking to an address, a corner, a park, a bar, life can spin on a dime.

You can stop for a doughnut and end up living in another country.

ODALISQUE

I once had a job as a nude model for a painter. Not just some guy in a studio who was playacting, but a great painter. A grand, absolutely eccentric, obsessed painter; a bit of a genius, with the occasional chilling gaze of the true monomaniac.

"Art should have a smell, a *smell!*" he'd say, ranting from behind his easel. "Because then, if it was bad, no one would have it in their house!"

"C'mon, give me a painting." (I was always whining.)

"Give you a painting? Give you a *painting?* Do you know how important a good painting is? Do you know how much a good painting is *worth?*"

"Well, give me a bad one, then."

"No. I can't do that."

"Why not?"

"Because the bad ones are my *enemies!*"

He worked on the Upper West Side of Manhattan in a huge skylit studio with jazz on the radio. The whole place was filled with an empty, quiet light. That studio was the safest place I've ever been, which is strange

13

considering I was buck naked on a large table piled with old bedspreads. I was really conscious of being really *naked*. Feeling all breasts and skin and hair with someone, with a *man*, staring intently at me, brushes in his hand, lunging at the canvas. It was great! I was actually part of the art as it was happening. Like being a piano or a toe shoe.

In his studio I felt beautiful. And I really loved being beautiful. Not just pretty, like a girl at a table at a fancy restaurant wearing a size six dress, laughing, her wineglass raised to her lips as her eyes flicker to see who else is watching. But beautiful. Beautiful.

Like a woman in a painting.

WHO AM I TODAY?

I got my first job when I was twelve years old. It was at Berkoff's Hardware Store on Coney Island Avenue. I'd gone in with fake working papers and told them it was illegal to have a sign that said BOY WANTED. They gave me the job: cleaning toilets. But what I really did was moon around the stock room waiting for Barney the stock boy to notice me. He was thick. He was hairy. He was stupid. He was sixteen. He had a shag haircut and I loved him.

Imagine being so young that you want to be older. When I was thirteen and a half I got a job at an Italian fast food place in a mall. A full hour from my house, I was anonymous, able to create the mnemonically perfect scenario necessary to lie about my age. I hung out with girls in cars and froze my face so I wouldn't utter gasps of disbelief at the shocking bits of information so casually revealed to me. This was glamour. This was nights out in Manhattan, in loud discos, dancing the hustle. I gave my mother some of my salary but with the rest I would buy wonderfully trashy clothes: wrap halter dresses, a red crepe pantsuit with a peplum. And shoes. Shoes that were made of apple-green wood, cantilevered high—as high as a step—with clown-colored straps that converged into a big white dot on the center of my foot. In the 1970s those shoes cost one hundred dollars. My mother freaked out. But up on those shoes I was grown-up. I was somewhere else. I couldn't believe I was worthy to own *those shoes.*

The promise of the shoes was fulfilled. I became a makeup artist for Helena Rubenstein at Bloomingdale's during the glory days of pure excess. The days when entire menageries were set up on the main floor with phalanxes of dancing girls, bushels of rose petals—all for the launch of a new perfume. Each day I changed out of my girls'-school uniform and transformed myself into an overpainted salesgirl.

Behind the counter we stood, arrogant, aloof, wearing fashionable masks of concealer, base, foundation, blush, powder, eyeliner, lip-liner, gloss, our bizarre and perfect faces turning slowly, our Etruscan smiles fixed while we murmured, "Everyone is using cream blush. *Everyone.*"

I was deeply blasé. I mean, I knew girls who were in their twenties. And from France. You see, at first there's the allure of alternative identities through employment. Then one day the wind shifts and you're a runaway living in a garage and you *have* to get a job.

BLOWN SIDEWAYS THROUGH LIFE

So you wake up every morning and you think, Who am I today? Who am I today? Who do you need? Today I'm a bartender at Imperial China Restaurant. I'm that. Or a proofreader at Bear Sterns. I'm that. I'm the takeout cook at the Exotica World of Gourmet with its kitchen opening onto a yard strewn with dog shit. I'm the translator for an Italian pop music band. A brunch chef on Fire Island. I'm Mrs. Rip van Winkle in the Centenary Parade of the Brooklyn Bridge. I'm that. I'm a hatcheck girl at a business-lunch restaurant. The fake secretary for a guy pulling a con involving pens.

Another day I'm a room service waitress for the Harley Hotel in New York. The only woman, the only non-Hispanic. The day starts at five A.M. when I put on a uniform, then ride in a huge elevator with a cart piled with giant trays. The elevator stops and a couple of other waiters, smiling encouragement, help me to heave the tray onto my shoulder. I stagger down the corridor, chanting the room number "Two fourteen. Two fourteen. Two fourteen." At last, there's the door. The tray weighs a ton. My arms are shaking. Somehow I manage to ring the bell.

Bing bong. "Room Service." (Oh God oh please oh God oh please don't let me drop the tray.) I hear

17

sounds of a shower through the door. (Oh God oh please.)

"Out in a minute!"

Finally the door opens and I careen into the room. "Goodmorninggoodmorningroomservicehere'syour breakfast!"

BOOM! The tray is down.

Back to the kitchen for the next one.

How much for the day? One hundred dollars? I'll do it.

Job for a catering company in a huge warehouse preparing lunch for a convention at Madison Square Garden: I'm wearing a hairnet and a huge plastic apron, up to my elbows in processed turkey in vats of brine. Great spheres of processed turkey meat encased in a rind of fat and gelatin wedge painfully under my fingernails as I lean over to lift them out. The brine stinks and leaves the floors and tables slick with grease.

I took a shower that night that lasted for an hour and a half.

You always have to say yes to get a job. Never have a personality, a life, a light, an opinion. And just yes isn't good enough. You have to *smile* at some cock-sucker in a cheap suit engorged with the majestic power to hire and fire. And if you don't, it means you have a bad attitude.

A bad attitude?

He can't imagine my attitude.

What I really want to do is grab him by his swirly tie and scream, "I'd like to smack you so hard your whole fucking family would cry! I'd like to kick you to death in front of your dog!" Those are the times when you can't take it. When to smile and say yes makes you feel like your mouth is packed full of sand and shit.

Still, it's *great,* that moment when you get the job. Great, that moment of the first paycheck. All too soon, though, there's that clench in the stomach as the dreaded punch-in, sign-in, be-on-the-floor time approaches. And as you walk to the first table, pick up the first document, push the button to take the first call, you think, I'll never get through this. And then you finally finish your shift and it's time for the late-night ride in the taxi, counting your cash by the streetlights.

Sitting down after hours on your feet is as pure as drinking water, as satisfying as biting into an apple. You're too fired up to go to sleep, so you sit at the kitchen table. It's late. It's quiet. You're tired. But you don't want to go to bed. Going to bed means this was the day. This February twelfth, this August third, this November second, is over. You made some money but nothing happened. Nothing. A whole day of your life is over, and all it means is that it's time to go to bed; a moment at four o'clock in the morning when you

19

think that life is too hard, the tasks are impossible. There is no Grail. There is no treasure. The only talismans that protected me were the constancy of books and the comfort of food. Until I was really well read and over two hundred pounds. "The human sofa!" I joked, because I wore a gray skirt made out of upholstery fabric.

I wore it every day.

BUSTER KEATON WAS MY
BOYFRIEND

That year, the year of the skirt, was the year that Buster Keaton became my boyfriend. In my journal I wrote pages of pure longing, even poems that had lines from things like Joni Mitchell songs ("What a sorry face you get to wear . . ."). I was really alone that year. My family wouldn't talk to me. I had moved out of a garage into an apartment on a slummy street with a bag of laundry and a box of Mallomars. I worked crappy jobs and went to a college that was like a cruel joke, where people slumped in chairs asked, "Do we *have* to read the whole book?" In one English class there was a row of guys who sat in the back of the room. "Oh, here comes Shakespeare!" they would scream when I walked through the door. In response I would turn slowly in my seat and stare at them impassively, blinking, in silence, sure I had crushed them. I was sure because at those moments I thought I looked like Keaton, that I had the force of his gaze.

One night I'd gone to a theater in Greenwich Village

that was having a silent-film festival. There, I saw my first Keaton film. The first shot of his face opened something inside me. His face had the etched perfection of a classical statue and the liquid, compassionate eyes of a Perugino Madonna. His eyes—in his baby pictures, his films, even as an old man—were always the same. He was so beautiful, so graceful.

The film I saw was a short film from 1922, a two-reeler called *Cops*. Buster is trying to make good to win the girl he loves. A dizzying sequence of mishaps follows as each of Buster's plans goes awry, mishaps that ultimately lead to a shot of an empty street, a deserted world. And then, far off, at the farthest point, is a lone figure: Buster. Running. I had never seen anyone run like Keaton—perfectly coordinated, impossibly fast, his face blank in concentration. As he runs toward us the street suddenly fills with cops, waves of cops, a fantastic number of cops, bearing down on the swift but doomed fugitive.

Here was my kindred spirit, who ran the way I ran in my dreams after I plodded through the day. I sat there in the sticky-floored theater, barely breathing, my popcorn forgotten (I never ate at a Keaton movie again), glaring at the screen in my hunger for detail.

I saw every Keaton movie, read every book, every article, not like some cineaste collecting facts and dates, it was just that anything about him was, well . . . about *him*. What women tell their lovers I told him in my heart. He was who I wanted and what I wanted to be. I was so afraid of being vulnerable or babyish or foolish and there was Keaton, continually thwarted and mocked by the world, sometimes looking sadder than I could bear, but holding fast to who he was, what he loved.

There is a moment in the beginning of the film *The General* where we see Buster as a young engineer standing by his locomotive, and he reaches over to the train car and delicately brushes off a tiny spot. This huge machine is known to him down to the smallest speck of dust. His was not just passion, but the pride of having a great love of something and being really good at it, even if no one else knew. In his films he was always misunderstood, the world mocked him, blind to his genius, his beauty—genius and beauty that *we* saw. This I could understand. This was me, wasn't it?

On Halloween that year (always my favorite holiday —no family things, no presents, just dressing up and candy) I went to a huge party dressed as Buster Keaton. I bought a man's suit in a thrift shop and tracked down a stiff collar, wore white makeup. I even found a porkpie hat. I must have looked bizarre. Imagine a short, extremely round, and very very pale young woman in a too-large suit, roaming around a room packed with festive costumes, looking into people's faces expectantly, sure that someone would get it.

23

No one, and I mean not one person, knew who I was. But I didn't care. I walked around that night in shoes too big, the collar digging into my chubby chin, dressed as someone else, but knowing who I was. Knowing that the world may have taken me for a fool, but that didn't mean the world was right, because, after all, look how wrong it had been before.

YOU WANT IT, BUT *THEY* GOT IT!

I'm wearing a nerdy skirt set that my friend's rich grandmother passed on, a classic ensemble that before this appointment has only done lunch. I'm in the ubiquitous pastel, plasterboard waiting room of an employment agency trying to think up dates so that my résumé doesn't look made up. Oh, the elaborate lies I've told: "Yes, of course. I worked a computer like that for six months." "Uh, yes. I'm very familiar with cappuccino machines." Great misshapen lies that stink as they hit the open air while I lift my eyebrows quizzically and smile a friendly smile that shows how simple it is to work with me, what a swell person I am to hire. Easy, that's me! Easy and on time.

Work every weekend? Sure. Work a computer, a register, a switchboard? Sure. Work until four A.M. and drag the bar mats out to the street and hose them down? Sure. The interviewer behind today's desk is the Grand Inquisitor and you, my friend, are on the rack.

25

Still, if I get the job I'm thrilled. *I got a job and I will make some money and I can buy a book on the way home!*

Then, the new boss launches into a litany: You have to be here an hour early for side work. . . . You pay if there is any breakage. . . . Punch in and out for your lunch. . . . Punch in and out for your break. . . . We allot about a half hour per document. . . . You are responsible for your shirt, your jackets, your knives, your pens. . . . And always: Such and such and this and that are GROUNDS FOR IMMEDIATE DISMISSAL.

A horror film begins inside my head. Behind my benign, helpful, supplicant gaze is the hoarse muttering of an unrestrained maniac waving a straight razor at the thought of coming to work tomorrow morning.

There is nothing worse than the first day on a new job. Always you a) didn't sleep well the night before, b) are starting some kind of tedious minor illness like a bladder infection or a mouth-breathing head cold, c) having a fight with your 1) mother, 2) boyfriend, 3) neighbor next door. You arrive and watch as every other employee rushes past you, knowing where they are going. A bizarre rictus forms and *your face stays that way for the rest of the day* as you follow the manager, the supervisor, the headwaiter, the floor manager, bobbling your head, trying to look as though every word you are hearing is sinking in.

But nothing is sinking in because your brain will not shut up. Oh, I'm gonna hate this, I'll never be able to a) lift that pot, b) remember to check that document, c) stay up until four A.M., d) not freak out when all the lights on that console start flashing.

They are really easy on you that first day. They give you perks that you will kill for in a few weeks and *you will never see again.* The first day you get to a) order from the menu, b) sit on a chair while you check reservations, c) leave your bow tie in your bag, d) get off early.

The second day is despair.

AFRICAN DANCE

Changing into my tights in the cold employee toilet two afternoons a week, in flight from my job of the week, I'm on my way to an African dance class. The studios in the old loft building are ancient. The barres pull free unexpectedly, their nails slipped loose from crumbly walls pocked with previous attempts at security. The floors are worn smooth, soft as old sheets, imbued with innocent sweat and the sweet stink of wood.

Charles, our teacher, stands before us, ageless in his silver-gray leotard, every muscle in his body as defined as a medical illustration, every rope and twist clearly seen.

"Dance like you have a big jewel of your grandma's right in the middle of your collarbone"—his voice rings out as the drummers in the corner begin their beat—"and you want evvveryone to see it!" A ball peen hammer in one long, spatulate hand, stooping to bang back a nail that had sprung free from a loose floorboard, Charles would cajole us with positions, directions. "Don't look at your friends!" he orders. "Your friends are *wrong!*"

We line up, two by two, panting and nodding to our partner, our bodies rocking in one-two-three hesitation, like preparing for the entering leap into a moving jump rope.

"Second second first-and-turn! Second second first-and-turn! Second first and NEXT GROUP!"

I move out to the floor, it's my turn to dance, and as I go the world comes down to a plié and a turn and sometimes, sometimes I get the step, I'm really dancing, and how old I am or what my thighs are like or where I have to go afterward or where I was before doesn't matter. The office fluorescent is sweating itself out of my pores, the work is forgotten. I am in the land of the body where time is only the measure of the music.

One of the drummers begins to chant and now everyone is whooping, ululating, and even Charles begins to dance, his body transformed into a great avian swoop, head tilted on his long neck, arms stretched out like wings. When he starts to move the drums become thunder and we all go wild and the room is contained cacophony until the last couple dances across the floor and the music stops.

The class is over.

It's time to go back to work.

IN THE TRENCHES

Waitering. What a way to make a living. It's prison, voluntary incarceration, as we line up in the kitchen at three P.M. for the "family meal," pushing our trays along, food dumped on our plate at each station. One of the waiters jokingly asks for "a breast, please, Warden!" and the line of guys in white shirts and ties, order books in breast pockets, shout with laughter. I am the only woman. The man's uniform shirt is too large, the slim-cut khakis are stretched tight over my huge butt. I look incongruous. I look costumed.

Waiters are always hungry. We start work at three P.M., force down the shitty staff meal, then pump ourselves up at the espresso machine with tiny heavy cups of black nervous energy. By ten P.M. we'd kill for a bite of whatever the Vodka-Stinger lady with epaulets on her designer jacket is pushing around her plate. See us turning aside nonchalantly as we leave the kitchen, ducking behind the door to snatch the shrimp, pop the roasted potato. It's too hot, so what? The guy who cuts up the fancy overpriced pizza sneaks me a slice and I share it with my busboy in a corner, the two of us wolfing it down, laughing and moaning. My friend Regina once purloined a small round Buffalo mozzarella, and as she put it in her mouth the manager came up behind her so she swallowed it whole. For days afterward, she said, she could feel the ball of cheese working its way through her body.

Waitering brings a kind of hilarity I have never found in any other kind of job. Perhaps it's because the level of stress is ridiculous in proportion to what is actually happening: Dinner is being served. Or perhaps it's because an unusual range of people waiter: Aspiring actors work alongside people who are supporting families alongside dedicated party animals who love the hours and the cash. Unusual *people* waiter. My friend Bill, a young actor, worked in a French restaurant. One night, while waiting at the bar, he overheard Barbara, the bartender, ask one of the other waiters, a French guy named Pierre, to get her some milk from the kitchen for a cocktail.

"Oh. Please. No!" Pierre pleaded.

"What? I'm swamped. Just get me some milk!"

"I am so sorry, Barbara," Pierre said regretfully, shaking his head, "but I really cannot."

"Why not?" Barbara demanded. But Pierre just backed away, waving one hand woefully.

"Will someone please tell me what is going on?" Barbara asked one of his compatriots.

"Well," another waiter said as Bill and Barbara leaned toward him, "Pierre, he has a problem. He is scared of milk."

"*Scared* of milk?"

"He cannot touch milk. It makes him afraid to be near it."

Bill and Barbara are beyond normal laughter.

"It is serious," the waiter said. "He truly has fear of milk . . . and carrots."

Dave was my favorite waitering partner. He was very, very tall, almost six feet seven inches tall, and he towered over everyone in the dining room, wading through the crowds of diners and busboys like Gulliver moving through a sea of Lilliputians. He had a perfectly sculpted face and an unusually sonorous voice—he'd trained to be an opera singer. Dave was dangerous to be stationed with because he would, in a perfectly clear, audible voice, make comments that would have you running into the kitchen to cough and sputter with laughter. Amazingly (perhaps because he did it with such aplomb) the customers never noticed.

There was a customer—Marianne something—who always sat in our station, the "VIP" station, tables number thirty-two to thirty-eight. She was an overthin older woman in fashion-victim outfits of busy jackets and accessories. "Molto VIP," the manager would mutter as she came through the door. VIP or not, she was a waiter's nightmare of special requests and petulant sighs of displeasure.

"Molto VIP Marianne, her mother died a few months ago," the manager told us one night after he had seated her, "and she is very sad."

Not too sad to send back the wine and want the bread heated.

I stepped up to her table and began laying menus in preparation for Dave to take her order. Suddenly he was slowly revolving around her table, eyes cast heavenward, beginning to moan in a ghostly, sobbing voice: *"Whooo whooo Marianne* it's your mother *whooooo . . ."*

I tried to firmly ignore him by setting the fish knives and pouring the water.

". . . whoooo whoooo Marianne order the pizza *whoooooo* the fish isn't any good . . ."

I dropped the water pitcher on the table with a thud, then ran to the kitchen, wheezing with laughter until Dave glided in and we fell on each other. Seconds later the manager arrived screaming, "Your entire section, abandoned!" With suitably penitent expressions we bustled back to the dining room, and for the remainder of the night, when we passed each other, we'd make soft hooting sounds then burst into giggles.

"Hey," a customer said as we served him, "you must really like your jobs!"

Out on the floor it's the front lines, it's a war, and the waiters are caught between two flanks—customer and management. Comrades-in-arms, we share a look across a table, shield each other from the manager as we surreptitiously pry a broken cork out of a wine bottle. We are in this together. Sneaking down to the employee bathroom to share a cigarette, we curse the customers, or repeat the joke of the week ("Christ, I feel like Papillon, I should shove my tip money up my ass"). Back on the floor, during a lull, we lean against a wall and engage in "waiter conversation": two people side by side but never looking at each other, mouths hardly moving, eyes scanning the room for the lift of a beckoning hand.

You are expendable, the smallest slip can lead to the freefall of unemployment. Survival is all.

Tips for Waiters

1. Avoid the "family meal." At all costs, eat before you go to work. I once waitered at a place where every night they served bloody chicken legs, wilted salad, and crunchy pasta with acidic tomato sauce. For months.

35

2. Wear cop shoes. As a waiter your entire consciousness is centered in your feet. Cop shoes are strong, cheap, and give you a certain clomping authority.

3. Get retractable pens. You'll lose the top to any other kind, get Rorschach stains on your uniform shirt, and your manager will force you to buy a new one.

4. Get the best busboy. Bribe him if you must.

5. Avoid the VIP tables. Waiting on Warren Beatty is far more trouble than it's worth. At first it's kind of a thrill, but then it's just another table that wants more water and bread, wants to hear the "specials" again, only worse, because the manager is breathing down your neck, dying for an excuse to meet a star.

Tips for Customers

1. Never touch the waiter. Even if you think you are being nice, that you have a great rapport, think how shocking it would be if the waiter touched *you*.

2. Don't ask personal questions. I've been asked questions by customers that even my mother wouldn't ask me.

3. Order dinner without commentary. We aren't interested if you like chicken, hate carrots, never eat white flour. Simply tell us what you want.

4. Finish chewing before you talk to the waiter. We'll wait. Really.

5. Don't snap your fingers.

6. Don't call the busperson "Pedro" or "Ahmed" or "Consuelo." Or any other name you think might be his or hers because of nationality.

7. Don't mention the tip. As in "Listen, take good care of us and you'll get a really good tip."

8. Don't complain to the manager. Restaurants are tough places, so know that if you complain, it means the subject of your criticism will be fired. FIRED. Out the door. Now, we're talking about a dinner you ate balanced against a person's job.

ON THE WAY TO WORK

Climbing the dunes of subway steps up and out, the crunch of trash underfoot sounds like sand, the concrete glints and hints at treasure. Waves of traffic roar above the gull-like screeching of braking cars. Young boys in low-slung, baggy pants bob and weave through the crowd. Bike messengers flash like neon fish. The sky is the same, I guess, as the sky over the sea. Navigating the streets, crossing the current, you make the light, catch the bus. If you get the rhythm of a day in the city you can run before the wind.

Stopping for a moment to wait for the light to change on the corner, you lift your face, get your bearings, see the sun or see the moon, check out the neighborhood. Compared to Inside, the street is so lovely, it hurts.

On your way to work, a city street is like a beach in Paradise.

HOT KNIFE THROUGH BUTTER

Job followed job in syncopation. Getting a job. Quitting it. Getting a job. Quitting it. Getting a job. Getting fired. Getting a job. Getting fired. As the time span of jobs shortened, the quality of jobs decreased. From the kind of jobs where you fill out an application form, to the kind of jobs where a guy pays you with cash pulled from his pants pocket. I went through jobs like a hot knife through butter. I went through butter like a hot knife through butter. I was really stoned all the time. I was really fat all the time.

Being fat is the absolute nadir of the misfit. You're a misfit because nothing fits. You don't fit in. You're not fit. You're fat. Fat doesn't have the poetic cachet of alcohol, the whiff of danger in the drug of choice. You're just fat.

Being fat is so un-American, so unattractive, unerotic, unfashionable, undisciplined, unthinkable, uncool. It makes you invisible. It makes you conspicuous. You, standing at the kitchen window, looking down into the street, forehead pressed against the

41

glass, watching a girl who's all dressed up on a Saturday night get into a car and drive away and you're crying because you're fat.

I went into freefall. I slipped between the cracks. The center did not hold. My rule book was lost. I'd been fired once too often. The ecstasy of relief of the job left, the orgasm of the nasty retort spoken turned sour, as the fear beneath began to mutter, Oh, what am I gonna do? What's gonna happen to me? My chest is like a fist. I have no money. Oh, shit, I really did it this time.

Walking down the street I saw myself in a store window. And I stopped. I couldn't believe that what was inside me looked like this to other people, that *this* was what the world saw: me, slumped and sloppy, my hem dipping between pins, my body layered with defeat. When I was a child I used to lie in bed and arrange my body so that it was in the exact pose as the figure on my Brownie cap, a capering figure airborne in an ecstatic moment of body and space.

Panic grew. I'll be all right I'll be all right. I won't go under. That's the unthinkable. Poor isn't about "not having," poor is about fear. So I'd meet a friend and smoke a joint on a bench in the park. Or stand in the peace of a bookstore and read in the aisle. It's so nice not to be working. (It's so horrible to be out of a job.) I can do anything I want today. (I don't have any money.)

42

Talking about the situation gives it a glow, though. Failure reflected back as danger. The shudder of black leather, of the East Village, of facial flesh pierced with rings. I felt proud. I felt cool. I could do this. I could live through this. Mine was the cocksure glance of the handcuffed as they're led to the van. The fucked-up romance of watching TV shows about hospitals when no one really wants to be in one.

This is how I got a job in a whorehouse.

"FIVE VERY PRETTY
GIRLS"

I got a job as a phone girl in a whorehouse on East Forty-ninth Street. On Halloween night. I went for my interview to an anonymous, ugly East Side building and emerged from the second-floor elevator to the smell of cleaning fluid and heavy perfume. The door was opened by a girl wearing gym shorts and basketball sneakers. She led me past the living room, which was very Bloomingdale's-furniture-floor-show-room: smoked mirrors and sectional sofas. Then she showed me into a tiny, shabby office. The walls were grimy white with unexpected smears of color from someone's lipsticky finger. Stuck up with curls of dirty Scotch tape was a poster of a guy with one foot propped up on a Rolls-Royce that said POVERTY SUCKS. Behind a cheap wooden desk sat an immense young woman wearing a clown suit and a red rubber nose. She was so fat that the arms of her chair had been worn down to the foam by the friction of her enormous ass as she got in and out of the seat. She, Lori, had an incongruously tiny voice. A girly giggle voice.

The perfect phone-girl voice. I'd thought that a smoky Bacall murmur would be the way to go, but no.

Lori ran the place for Steve the Pimp. She was in charge of dividing about fifteen girls between the day and evening shifts, scheduling the afternoon cleaning guys, ordering supplies of toilet paper and mouth-wash, and hiring and firing. She hired me for three nights, two days, at fifty dollars a shift plus five dollars for each booking. A booking was a "session": a girl or girls in a room with a man for half-hour or hour incre-ments. Basically, I was a pimp too. If the place had been busted the girls would just be fined, but I would have been in the deepest kind of shit because solicit-ing over phone lines is a federal offense.

Each day I would get off the Lexington Avenue local and stop at the bakery for a bag of treats, then drop by the tiny used-book store on the same block. The bookstore man was a sweet-faced fellow, but not all there. While hunting through the yellowing paper-backs, choosing the handful of books that would get me through my shift, I'd make conversation with him, a connection, for a moment, of innocence before work.

I dreaded going into the building. If other tenants got on the elevator, my stomach would clench in an-ticipation of their flinty looks, their mutterings of "whore" as the elevator door closed behind me. Then, trudging down the stinky hallway, I would ring the bell, wait for an eye to appear in the peephole and a voice to say, "Who is—? Oh, it's you," and the door to swing open.

The shift begins: I set down my stuff in the office, check out the number of sessions on the legal pad to see how business is, to see which girls are on, and to check with them about where we were going to order dinner. I sit down at the prefab desk, line up the two phones, straighten the cord for the wall phone (the private line), and reach for the desk phone as it, inevitably, begins to ring.

Each shift was eight hours. Five or six girls worked each shift. Hanging out with me they would sprawl on the stained sagging furniture, smoking, talking, looking at magazines and menus. Swallowing a bit of brownie, a bite of chocolate, I'd try to pick up the phone and do my rap without losing the thread of a conversation, the place in my book: "Hi we have five very pretty girls two brunettes a redhead and two very busty blondes it's ninety-five for the hour seventy-five for the half hour that includes French and straight coming twice in the hour and once in the half hour. Gotta pen? . . . Yes the redhead is very beautiful she's an ex-cheerleader"—(I twist my mouth at Pamela, who flaps her hands limply in the air and mouths, *Rah rah*—)"Garter belts are extra you can talk about it with the girl"—(me nodding yes as Doris mimes *Wanna soda?*)—"The brunette is athletic and

47

the blonde is very busy . . . oh, a thirty-eight D. Gotta pen?" I'm always asking if they have a pen because if they write down the address it's likely they'll show up. Again the phone rings and I grab it without looking up from my book, say the rap without thinking.

Soon the buzzer rings from downstairs and the group starts moaning.

"Oh, *you* get it! I got it the last time." One of the girls gets up, grudgingly, and presses the intercom in the wall.

"Hi!"

"Uh, hi. It's John. . . . I called?"

"Oh, sure, John"—rolling her eyes—"c'mon up."

Everyone stands, adjusting bras and hair and putting on spiky shoes. Mardi Gras in midtown. Jenny, wearing little gym shorts and a teeny T-shirt; Marie, decked out in a long dress and heels and so much under-eye cover cream that she looks like a raccoon; Robin in a white minidress, ruched up on the seams like a theater curtain. "It's a wallet, girls!" one of them mutters, as "John" is escorted to the living room.

The girls sit around him in the "conversation pit," ask him about movies or baseball. But never, never, do they mention money or sex.

Sometimes we'd buzz a guy in and he'd try to be cool. "Hey!" he'd say, swaggering. "How much is a blowjob?"

"We only discuss sports and the weather," one of the girls would answer sweetly.

If he persisted with such questions, everyone was sure he was a cop and played really stupid until he left.

Normally, though, the group sits there for a few minutes, some of them, like Robin, making no effort whatsoever, just sitting there smoking, swinging a crossed high-heeled foot. Peering out from the hinged crack of my door I try to see what the guy looks like so I can be part of making fun of him when they all troop back in.

Finally, the guy chooses and he and the girl walk to one of the five rooms. (There were two bedrooms down the hall, a bedroom upstairs reached by a strangely pitched spiral metal staircase, and two studio apartments down the hall. We were the entire second floor.) Once there, the girl would stand by the door and say the following: "Make yourself as comfortable as the day you were born." Translation: "Be completely naked when I get back or I'll think you're a cop and throw you out." Then the girl would return to the office to sign the room out on my legal pad. That way I could make sure she was only working for the time specified. She'd hang out for a while, waiting for "John" to undress and, hopefully, to wash.

In all the romanticizing about whoring—the Happy Hookers, the Pretty Women—people's personal hy-

49

giene, their really distinct smell and taste, is never touched upon. Once a girl named Tiffany made me laugh as she described cajoling a big fat guy into the shower. "But he didn't fucking wash, you know? He just let the water run over him. So instead of a smelly fat guy, I got a *wet* smelly fat guy." Before the girl goes back to the room, she counts the rubbers in her little zip bag—every girl there had one—and borrows garter belts or stockings if she needs them. Now she's ready.

On a good night, when a John wanted a "double" (two girls at once), I'd be all alone in the office and when the doorbell rang I'd have to answer it myself. Answer it in my greasy sweatpants, a yachting cap pulled low over my face. "Someone will be right with you," I'd hoarsely mutter, then stomp back to my room, trying to give off extremely negative, dangerous vibes as I shut the door, my heart thudding because I was afraid. Because I was ashamed.

On the other hand, if it was a slow night, and everyone was lazy and cranky, I would get really pushy. Particularly at Karen, a dazed girl with huge breasts and thin, wispy blond hair that she combed compulsively, hypnotically, but she was very popular because of, well . . . big tits, blond hair. The best seller.

"Go out! Go out!" I'd encourage her if the buzzer rang. "You look great! You're gonna get picked!" I wanted that five dollars.

BLOWN SIDEWAYS THROUGH LIFE

Once a girl was picked, everyone else would troop back into my office, lighting cigarettes, eating leftover takeout food. When I wasn't answering the phone, I would tell them stories, and sing, and do bits of Shakespeare. They thought I was silly, but that's what I wanted. To play the fool. To take the edge off the fact that I was there, but I wasn't turning tricks. It also helped that I was huge and dysfunctional, hunched at my desk with bags of candy and stacks of books, compulsively reading and eating, turning pages with chocolate-sticky hands and chewed fingernails, my slumped obesity a bizarre contrast to my chirpy phone voice.

"Is this any way to run a whorehouse?" I'd scream, swiveling in my chair, waving my legs in the air.

"You bet it is!" they'd scream back, laughing.

I envied the girls, envied them because they were thin, because they dressed up and wore lipstick and guys liked them. Robin was my favorite. She was twenty, with reddish-blond hair worn in a disco blown-dry style. She had amazing round breasts. She showed me the fine white scars from the implants. I was fascinated. She never hurried, never raised her voice. She walked with a swing, a complete movement of not just forward motion, but a deliberate footstep that led to an undulating of her hips. This was the sexiest walk I've ever seen. She had a tight, tough little Irish face, scowly and gruff. I was always trying to

51

make her laugh. Every once in a while I'd get her, and she'd let out this rusty, hesitant bark, a deep "hunh" of laughter, and her whole face would alter. She had a little dimpled smile with tiny white Chiclet teeth. For that rare flash of sweetness I would crow with glee.

Robin got into the whoring business the very night she and a friend came up to New York from somewhere down South. A young black guy picked them up at Port Authority Bus Terminal and took them out and bought them clothes and got them high. He must have been new at it, because the first time he left them on a street corner they just cut out and he never saw them again.

Then Robin hooked up with a guy who wasn't new at it. She said she tried to get away from him but she couldn't, until one night in an SRO hotel, she waited until he was asleep and then, barefoot, her boots in her hand, she crept down the stairs to the lobby. He must have heard her leaving because he caught her by the door and started beating her. "He kept hittin' me," she told me, "right here"—pointing to a puckered scar under her left eye. "He kept hittin' me and he had this big ring on and finally some guys pulled him off me and I thought I was gonna go blind." She finally got away from him one night when he passed out cold from drinking.

Soon after, she met JoJo in a bar. He was with the merchant marines and his uniform impressed her. He was good to her, though. He would leave her money on the dresser when he went away, but she still kept on hooking. After a while he got used to the life of late nights and short days and started living off her earnings. It happened like that a lot. At first the boyfriends worked, but they didn't have big-money jobs. So if they'd stayed out late doing cocaine, going to clubs, and spending a few hundred dollars, they thought what the hell. The progression from appreciating the money, to expecting the money, to demanding the money, is a quick one. So a pimp is born.

Gloria was tall and thin with a beaky nose and long dark hair she blew back and sprayed into two perfect rolls around her face. She wore lavender bell-bottoms from Frederick's of Hollywood and a tight ribbed top; the same outfit all the time, always clean, always neat. Gloria must have been a great housekeeper; she brought in salads in Tupperware containers and did needlepoint with images of frisky puppies and gamboling kittens. Commandeering the big armchair in the living room, she would sit with her legs crossed for hours at a time without moving, like the old ladies on Greyhound buses who ride through six states calm and upright with their purses on their laps.

Gloria was from Queens. She'd punctuate her speech with "Right?" (pronounced "Rye-eet?")—an upward inflection enhanced by a little dip of her chin. Every three words.

"How did I get started, right? Well, we used to swing, right? And Bobby"—her boyfriend—"said why not try hooking once, right? It'll be kinky, right? You can tell me all about it after, right?" Bobby would come by every night and stand on the corner and wait for her to finish a shift.

Most of the girls kept their personal lives a big secret, especially if they lived in a regular home, or had a double identity. But there were women like Kathy, for instance, who lived in a sleazy hotel and had lost touch with the real world. She would come out of a session and flop on the sofa, her blouse half buttoned, her jeans undone. Even when she became pregnant she never really discussed it; she just kept on working. The world she lived in was this world, the whorehouse world. She had no need to spend her money on the Charles Jourdan shoes and Vuitton bags that were the indicators of "class" to the world outside.

Kathy's mother and little sister also worked at the house. The three of them would do tricks together if that was what a guy wanted. Her little sister, Debbie, told me how they all started. How her mother pulled her into the car one night to go find Kathy because they heard she was hooking.

"We saw huh on da street," Debbie told me, "and she looked like uh clown. Huh face wuz all white, an' she had dese two red spots on huh face, like a clown. So my muthuh pulls huh inna car and starts beatin' on

huh, screamin', 'Youra hoowah! Youra hoowah!' "
"Yeah," Kathy says, holding up a fistful of fives, "but
look what I *made*!" So they all got into the act.

That year at Christmas Kathy gave me a green suede
belt trimmed with little gold beads. The belt wasn't
new, but I really liked it. That same Christmas I also
got a pair of gold pumps from a girl named Dee. She
didn't want them anymore, but I loved them. It had
been a long time since I'd had any dress-up clothes.
Dee was really petite, always very little-girl cute, even
among that group. But she had a huge heroin habit, so
she had fingers like sausages. Dee was extremely popular with the johns. "That's because she'll do *anything,*" the other girls would hiss. (The ultimate
putdown of a girl was that she either did it for free or,
worse, because she *liked* it.) Dee would keep a bottle
of bourbon in her black slouch bag, and by the end of
the night, if she took a trick to the upstairs room, we
would station someone at the foot of the stairs to help
her as she lurched down to the living room.

Suzanne was the other heroin fan. She was very
beautiful. Very tall. Very thin. Auburn bob. College
grad. Tasteful mocha trouser suits. Brooklyn Heights.
Never got picked.

My favorite times at the house were when we ordered in and the phones were quiet and the girls
would tell me of "in the rooms." "What do you do
with your face while some guy is fucking you?" was

55

the kind of thing I'd ask. "I just relax my face and half close my eyes" was the kind of answer I'd get. Then came stories of guys who draped their shirts over the lamp to make the room look more romantic, or tales of regulars like "Rubber Mike" who liked to drink out of used condoms. For him the girls would have to scurry around with a rubber, filling it with a mixture of milk, sugar, salt, and a little dash of bleach. There was a Japanese man who came to the house every Saturday morning at eleven A.M. with a bag of blueberry muffins for Pamela (he called her "Pamaya"), and a guy they called "Fourth of July" because he liked to lie on the floor and come into the air while a girl stood above him in white pantyhose. They showed me how you could put a rubber between your teeth and roll it down with your lips so you could put it on a guy while giving him a blowjob and he would never know.

Most of the stories had to do with getting away with something. Doing less and getting paid for it. Paid to lick some guy's butthole? Lick your forefinger and then flick it gently while making appropriate lapping sounds. Doing a double where the guy wanted the girls to go down on each other? Splay your hands over the other girl's crotch, but then just lick your fingers. During doubles one girl always tried to get behind the guy to make the other girl laugh. One day a guy came in and called all the girls into the living room. He then got up on the glass coffee table, stark naked on his hands and knees, as one girl masturbated him while he slowly revolved around on all fours. "Oh, look at you!" the others had to chant. "You're so big! You're so hot!" But as soon as they were out of his line of vision they began giggling and making faces. He paid them fifty dollars apiece to do this.

One Sunday morning we had a killer water-pistol fight that escalated into water warfare. Running through the rooms and screaming with glee were girls in spangly cheap clothing and sticky red lipstick, squealing and shooting water pistols like it was a summer afternoon on a tree-lined street. At night we'd order in from a barbecue place around the corner and have huge feasts of ribs and onion rings and iced tea (Robin's favorite) while sitting around the ratty office, steaming knots of tinfoil filled with hot fried food on our laps, groaning if the buzzer rang. We'd smoke joints in the downstairs bathroom and sit around giggling, making fun of Pamela, the redheaded cheerleader. She had a slight overbite, like Gene Tierney, so that when she took a drag of a cigarette it looked positively pornographic.

When I'd get bored on the phones I'd say stuff to the callers just to make everyone laugh.

"Uh, hi. Do you have any girls there with long fingernails?"

"No," I'd say matter-of-factly, "we're all nail-biters here."

"Hi, uh . . . Hi, uh . . . Whaddaya look like?"

"Um, I'm five foot three and I weigh about two hundred and fifty pounds and my hair's dirty."

Sometimes I'd pick up the phone and hear only silence, breathing, then "I'm cominggg. . . ."

"Good for you!" I'd say, encouragingly. "On the paper! On the paper!"

One guy called all the time. "I'd like to have a session," he began simply, in a singsong voice. He would then start the graphic descriptions of anal sex. His cadence was so unique, though, that I could pick up the phone, hear his voice, and hang up without missing a beat in my conversation, my book, my burger.

Picking up the phone, putting it down. Picking up the phone, putting it down. Being there made the rest of my life a watery limbo of Not There. If I worked a double shift, a Friday night and Saturday day, for example, I would spend the night at the house because it was too late to take the subway back to Brooklyn, where I lived (we would close at three or four A.M. and reopen at nine or ten the next morning). A young gay guy named Barry kept the place very clean, but I brought my own pillowcase to have something familiar and comforting.

After the girls left, each carrying a bag of incriminating garbage, I would lock the door and unplug the phones and go into the back bedroom on the first floor. There, I'd pull back the quilted polyester print bedspread and lie with my eyes open, telling myself not to be fanciful, to ignore the feeling that the air in the room seemed heavy with woe and loneliness and the chilly whiff of evil. I always had strange dreams there; when the alarm went off at eight A.M. I would wake up and realize I'd been crying. Sitting on the edge of the bed, wrapping my arms around my knees, rocking slightly, promising myself big cheesy Danishes and cups of coffee, I'd make myself get up. Get up and put on the sweatpants, plug in the phones, and hope Steve the Pimp didn't come in when it was still early and I was still without my shell.

Steve terrified me. He was a good-looking prepster, with fair hair and Brooks Brothers suits and flat, dead eyes. He was vicious, in the way that coke addicts are vicious, but a lot of it was just him. He would criticize the girls all the time. He'd tell them they were fat, or that they didn't pull in enough business. They dreaded the times when he'd take one of them into a room, because he would throw a pillow on the floor for their knees and then sit on the edge of the bed, pull out a popper, and curse at them while they tried desperately to make him hard. Impossible, it seemed; after a session with him they would come back into the office waving a pinky finger and rolling their eyes. Whenever Steve would come into the office I'd

59

lower my head so that my cap brim blocked my face and wonder if my friend's dad could ever imagine where his yachting cap had ended up and how it helped me.

"Are you stupid?" he'd say, flicking me on the arm. "Answer the phone before the third ring!"

"Yeah. You're right. I'm sorry," I'd say tonelessly.

One afternoon, tired of takeout, I was actually cooking homemade pasta sauce on the tiny, never-used stove when Steve came in and freaked out. "You fat bitch! Do you think we want this place to smell like a fucking kitchen! Homey? Cozy? *Shit!* Clean it up NOW!" I ducked my head and threw everything into the garbage.

I hated him. I hated that the girls had to pay him sixty percent of their earnings. So I came up with a scam and convinced a few of the girls to participate. I wouldn't sign in their session, and they would keep all the money and give me a twenty off the top. Then one of the girls told Lori, the manager. She called me at home. She threatened me. I laughed.

I got fired.

Well, I thought, I'd better get a job in another whorehouse. After all, the money was good. I could smoke pot and read and eat and I knew that any normal place I walked into for a job would never hire me, me with my lank hair and grotty clothes. So I bought *Screw* magazine and set up an appointment through their Help Wanted section—at a house on Forty-eighth Street and Lexington Avenue, up the stairs, above a deli. This house was much seedier. No living room. No beveled mirrors. Just one long hall with small rooms off each side.

When I got there I was buzzed in by an older woman in a greasy black dress who unsmilingly motioned for me to follow her down the hall. Walking behind her I looked into one of the rooms. No Holiday Inn decor here. Just a bare room and bed and a girl lying there, fully dressed, just staring at the ceiling. Down the hall the woman was waiting.

"Hi!" I say, stepping into the room. "I've worked as a—"

"Make yourself as comfortable as the day you were born and I'll be right back," the woman says.

"No, but . . . I'm here about the phone-girl job. . . ."

She steps out and shuts the door.

Oh, shit. What do I do? I guess she thinks I could be a cop. I CAN'T take off my clothes. I'm too fat. Oh, God, I need a job.

So I stepped out of my shoes and pulled down my sweatpants. And stood there, alone, half dressed, and

looked around me. Me. Alone. In a room in a whorehouse.

I pulled up my pants and pushed on my shoes and
walked out the door and down the hall. By the time I
got to the stairs I was running, until I found myself on
the street, and the street full of people going about
their normal day looked like a scene in a film happening in front of me. I walked slowly to the corner, to a
pay phone, stepping up to it to get out of the street
flow because I couldn't breathe. Hunched over the
little metal shelf I cried in great gulping sobs.

When I was a child I was like Lear. I'd thought, I
will do *such things*.

AMI L'AMORE

Determined to hide in the half-life of whorehouse jobs, I answered an ad for phone work from home. This took me to an address in the east fifties to meet Ami L'Amore. Ami looked to be about thirty years old. She had a grating, whiny voice and pale skin, blotchy from slept-in makeup. She ran her call-girl service from a tiny walk-up apartment, which was filled with crushed red velvet furniture covered with plastic slipcovers, and wall units of Moorish inspiration.

Pretending we could be friends, I sat on the plastic sofa and played with her dingy little poodle and gritted my teeth against the smell of bad perfume, crusty ashtrays, and dog urine from the stained daily tabloids pushed into a corner. Encouraged, she brought out a huge mounted photograph of herself, topless, posed artfully against a Greek column. (That photo stayed propped against the wall for the entire time I knew her.) Ami explained that her phone would be forwarded to my house while she and another girl would go to hotel bars to pick up men. When they were

63

successful, Ami would call me with the hotel room number and tell me the amount of time involved. I would call when the time was up to make sure all went well, et cetera, et cetera. Or, if a "client" called, my job would be to describe the girls available on that night, beep them, and send them to the guy's hotel room.

All night long she would call me, more and more drunk with each phone call, from the Plaza, the Vista, the Intercontinental. In between, sitting in my kitchen, I would talk to clients I'd never see about girls I'd never met based on Ami's particular pornographic descriptions.

Home, home, I was always home. Home, slumped in a chair, reading, reading. The only exceptions were the times I would sally forth in the day for provisions: great sacks of food and bags of books. Books from the library, paperbacks from wire drugstore racks, plastic-wrapped books sold from a table on St. Mark's Place, leather-bound books with the irregular edges of the days of the paper knife and desk blotter, old orange Penguin paperbacks still marked with shillings and pence.

Being home was all I ever wanted. I wasn't fat at home. I could wear binge clothes at home, great stained T-shirts, droopy sweatpants. I could cook and eat and read and no one would know. Standing at the kitchen window, bleary, bored, sad, I would stare down at the cars and people, flinching when the phone rang.

One afternoon, six months later, I picked up my weekly wad of fives and tens from Ami and began walking. I walked all the way downtown, through the emptying city, the neighborhoods changing, block after block. I walked all the way to the Lower East Side and it wasn't until then that I realized I was crying in a weird, chuckling sort of way.

When I got home I called Ami. It took me an hour on the phone to quit, but I did it. I had to go back to the world. This was the bravest thing I've ever done—to go back to a world I wasn't sure wanted me.

FAE

*Nel mezzo del cammin di nostra vita mi ritrovai
nella selva oscura.*

In the middle of my road I found myself in a dark
wood. Like Dante, in order to find my way I first
descended . . . descended into a fetid damp basement room near Times Square to work for an answering service. I even had my Virgil, my guide, in the
unlikely form of a six-foot black transvestite named
Fae. She was really big. Big face, big lips, big long red
fingernails. And she wore lots of red lipstick, heavy,
heavy pancake makeup that left dark rings on the inside of her shirt collars, and tight, tight jeans. She
lived in Harlem in a large apartment with a stereo in
every room and ten TVs.

Fae had kicked a big heroin habit, only to get
busted for a disability-insurance scam. She'd worked
in the government disability office with a friend who
issued checks to her; then they'd split the money. So,
at rock bottom, Fae got this job with a young Jewish

guy, Marty, who was starting an answering service. They took turns answering the phones and crashing on an old couch so they could be there twenty-four hours a day. Unlikely duo. Great friends.

Enter me, into this windowless room filled with lopsided, ratty office furniture. During the day it was just me and Fae. Together we would sit in front of an old black-and-white TV that would only focus if you touched it. We'd take turns balancing one toe on the antenna, staring at stupid movies until the toe-thing got too annoying and we'd turn it off. I worshiped her.

The clients worshiped her too. Doctors, lawyers, brokers, would call in for their messages and she'd pick up the phone and say things like "What! I have to do *what*? No no no, child, all I have to do is stay black and *die*. Now, let me ask you something. How big is your dick? Don't lie to Fae, now!" And she'd laugh and laugh and laugh and they'd eat it up. "Fae," they'd beg, "can I put my friend on the phone? Oh, Fae, would you curse at my friend please?"

When delivery guys would come from the coffee shop she'd say, "You! You see her hands?" Pointing at me. "You see how *small* her hands are? You know how *big* that would make your dick look?" And the guy would scurry away and I'd be mortified and she'd roar.

No one was safe.

Marty had a really big butt and half of it was always hanging out of his pants. I'll never forget the day he bent over a desk to pick up a pen and Fae said, "My *God*! Look at that fat ass! Some motherfucker would like to sink in that thing up to his neck!"

Fae would tell stories on herself too, like the one about the guy who delivered her Craftmatic bed and she gave him a blowjob so he would leave it there on credit. That was Fae.

"Clo," she said to me one day, "you gotta stop wearing that skirt. People are makin' fun of you."

"Oh, who gives a fuck!" I said. But inside I died.

Hunched over in the janitor's closet that stank of Ajax and filth, I'd smoke joints, then go back to the phones, dry mouthed and dazed. I was always miserable, always complaining: "I'm so fat. I'm so poor. Everyone is having more fun than me." And she would lean over her desk and tap one long red fingernail on the telephone and say, "It ain't all about *you*, Clo. It ain't that kind of party."

About a year after I left that job I called Fae. I never keep in touch with people from jobs—the relationships are real, but they're site specific. Still, from time to time I would call Fae. She'd had a stroke. She said she was okay, but her mouth was a little skewed. A few months later I called again to discover she'd had a second stroke. Maybe it was the hormones. She told

69

me that while she was in the hospital, very sick, she'd had a spiritual awakening. That after a lifetime of agony, of never being happy or satisfied, she decided to be what she was. A man.

"I'm Frank now," he said. "I'm very happy. You be happy, Clo."

70

"GOOD MORNING!
SHAKESPEARE FESTIVAL!"

When I was a teenager, I worked at Joseph Papp's New York Shakespeare Festival. It was the best job I ever had. I started as a volunteer and became a part-timer, working the switchboard, the archives, the late-night jazz bar, the press office. The Public Theater complex was the center of my universe. I knew every inch of the classic sandstone building, and every inch was fascinating: the great recessed windows where I hiked myself up to watch the downtown world go by, the eerie catwalks of iron grid high above a dimly lit, empty set, the rooms filled with great, leaning stacks of plays and plays and plays. Every play I saw was the best play. I cried at every curtain. I had no critical distance. Anyone who worked there, anyone who was a grown-up who actually worked in the theater, was my idol.

Crawling commando-style across the balcony of the Anspacher Theatre, I'd lie on my stomach, looking down at the top of Meryl Streep's head as she rehearsed, or sneak in just as the lights faded to hunch

71

illicitly on the back steps to watch Irene Worth, Raul Julia, Colleen Dewhurst for the twentieth time. I was so proud to be there. There, where even the office supplies were special because they were used to make theater. There, where it was cool to care, where it was chic to be passionate, where it was assumed you were involved. Just to answer the phone, to say "New York Shakespeare Festival," meant I was part of it. I was just a chubby teenager at the switchboard, yet Joseph Papp asked me what I thought of yesterday's reading, last night's opening. Joseph Papp, the only person I ever behaved for. The only boss I ever loved.

I could find that teenager again. Going backward to go forward. Back to the juggling of jobs now made bearable by shoestring productions of plays in dirty rooms up creaky flights of stairs. I wanted to be an actress. Back to church basements and cheaply carpeted studios, taking acting classes that ranged from people sitting on chairs in their underwear crying "Mommy" to seated circles whispering Shakespeare by candlelight. Everything that made me a misfit in the world made me right for the theater.

A job onstage is a striving to tell a story, a story that is about you as you tell it, and in a living moment of contradiction about the people who are watching it. Onstage is where you are *supposed* to talk, *supposed* to laugh or cry, and *never* just "do your job."

CASTING CALL
DANCERS/SINGERS/ACTORS
10/8 from 9:30AM—1 & 2—6PM at
John Houseman Theatre Center, Studio B,
450 W. 42 St., NYC

With my own yellow legal pad and a roll of tape, I arrive before anyone else and tape up a page with my name written third on the list. That way I wouldn't be called first, before the auditioners would have a chance to get warmed up, but I would still finish early enough to get to my current job on time. By eight o'clock in the morning, the skanky stairwell was crowded with all of us hopefuls, clutching our pictures and résumés that were paid for by countless hours of waitering, word processing, whatever.

When it's my turn I walk into the room where three people are seated behind a plastic table.

"What are you going to do for us today . . ." (quick look at my picture) ". . . Claudia?"

I sit down on a teetering folding chair and try to breathe, to relax my toes, my hands, to remember what my Shakespeare teacher said about the sonnet, what my acting teacher said about the monologue. After I finish, I can't remember what I did or how I did. I am convinced that the smiles and thank-yous have dripped pity and compassion. I wasn't even thinking about my job before, but I'm thinking about it now. I bolt out of the building with only fifteen minutes to get there.

Even if the audition went badly, though, even if you walk away chanting the post-audition refrain of "I sucked, I didn't take my time, I pushed, I wasn't 'in the moment,'" it doesn't matter. Because those five minutes, those twenty lines of Shakespeare, Chekhov, Kondoleon, McNally, are the best part of the day. For that brief flicker of time you were more yourself, oh, much more you, than the person who pushes in the token to ride the train, to serve the duck, to take a message, to wipe the counter.

And the stress of shifts altered, of truncated paychecks, of jobs found and lost continued:

EXPERIENCED BARTENDER WTD.
Evenings, Wall St. area.

A Chinese restaurant.

The moo-shu egg roll type with a tiny dark bar downstairs. The entrance to the bar consisted of two double doors emblazoned with two cartoony dragons. Not dragons of treasure and fantasy, but garish winged vermin of dark caves and greed. Next to the bar a jukebox played the same moronic songs over and over. One big favorite was *"They're coming to take me away ha ha hee hee ho ho to the funny farm where life is beautiful all the time . . ."* followed by the repetitive punch of *"Another one bites the dust!"* Thump. *"Another one bites the dust!"* Thump. *"Another one bites the dust!"* Thump. *"And another one down and another one down and another one bites the dust!"* Thump.

Starting at about six o'clock the older guys in ties lined up, hunched over the bar, muttering, "Dewar's and water, Dewar's and water." The younger guys would stand behind them with girls in shirtwaist silk dresses and painful dainty pumps (standing meant you didn't want to get drunk, you wanted to get laid), laughing and pushing and drinking and bopping to the beat of the music.

There behind the bar I would sometimes duck down and open a cabinet and stick my head in for sanctuary. Just to have my face hidden from view. Just for a minute.

Don't they wanna go *home?* I'd think. Aren't they *hungry?*

My bosses were two older Chinese men. They were okay, but in my daze of showing up for, putting up with, and getting out, I would confuse their names. Finally, when I confused them once too often, one of the guys patted my hand and said, "No, no. I'm

75

Benjamin. The fat one, yes? Now you remember, yes?"

Just the pat of his hand, the literal touch of kindness, made me shudder to keep in the tears.

Bye.

PHONE PERSON WTD.
Fast talker, good with people, $10/hr.

A con game.

I went to a white, featureless room on the Upper West Side. The only furniture was one plastic table and two molded plastic chairs. On the table, two phones and many large leather-bound corporate reference books (Dun and Bradstreets, et cetera). My boss was a young guy in pressed jeans and a wrinkly tie. He had a mustache that looked like a finely trimmed eyebrow. The con? Call a B-level manager in a small subsidiary of a large corporation, say, out in Latrobe, Pennsylvania (we looked up the names in the books), and pretend to be the secretary to the president. Mr. Big calling Mr. Underling. When Mr. Underling would hear Mr. Big's name, he or she would take the call. Of course.

"Hi, Mr. Underling. I'm calling from Mr. Big's office. . . . Yes. . . . He's wondering if you could do him a small favor? A young friend of his is graduating from Harvard. . . . Yes, it's terrific. . . . Well, this friend has a small stationery concession that he has to liquidate before he goes to graduate school? Mr. Big has bought some of the leftover stock and thought that . . . Why don't I let you speak with him?"

That was my job. Just get the guy on the phone and my boss would do the rest: selling him cartons of stolen pens.

After one day I quit. Maybe it was the lying. Maybe it was the mustache.

VERSATILE COOK WTD.
Good pay.

Chic downtown café.

My first night on the job the boss says, "Okay. Make linguini with white clam sauce," and *I can't get the clams open.* Sweating, straining, lacerating my hands, I finally looked up at him and burst into tears. He was very nice about it. So nice, in fact, that I suddenly realized he was trying to kiss me.

I guess they had to change the specials after I left.

EXP. BRUNCH CHEF WANTED
Fire Island Pines—start immed. Free room.

Exactly what the ad said.

I'd won a prize! I was going to the beach! I was in the land of lust and sun, finishing my shift, then running to huge "tea dances" at four in the afternoon. I didn't care that I was the only straight woman there. Everyone I worked with made me laugh until I snorted like a hog. I had so much fun.

Until I got fired by the asshole who ran the kitchen.

By this point I was so adept at being fired (I mean, I'd been fired a lot more times than this guy had ever fired anyone) that he was more nervous than I was. So I told him I couldn't leave until the end of the week. He consented in an awkward moment of guilt. Four days, three nights. Luxurious beach resort.

HATCHECK GIRL WTD.
Good appearance.

Tacky midtown restaurant.

I showed up in the only decent clothes I owned: a pair of blue wool thirteen-button navy pants, a well-pressed men's pajama shirt from a thrift store, and a beret. The waitresses, however, wore a leotard, stockings, high heels, and . . . that was all. I would take the men's hats and coats, keeping my face Buster Keaton neutral. *I would not be friendly.* I hated the men who sat there eating and staring at the girls' bodies as they struggled with trays and stretched to place drinks.

One week.

ACTORS WANTED.
One-day performance. $150.00.

A parade for the centenary of the Brooklyn Bridge featuring characters from the stories of Washington Irving.

I showed up in Brooklyn at five A.M. to discover that I was *Mrs.* Rip van Winkle.

Dressed like fools we were forced to *run* across the bridge's car lanes, car lanes paved with a nubby metal grid that dug into our feet with each step. We were chivied across by an Indian guy with a walkie-talkie calling, "Hurry, pipple, please, pipple, hurry!" Riding beside us was a guy with a pink neon beard dressed as a dwarf, looking down from the heights of a horse-drawn carriage calling, "Watch the doo-doo!"

The crowd gaped. They had no idea who we were. One of them pointed to the guy dressed as Ichabod Crane and yelled, "YO! It's Abraham Lincoln!"

We did get free lunch in some huge insurance-firm employee cafeteria. We stayed for hours, staggering shamelessly back to our cluttered smoky table with towering trays of free food as the coordinator watched uncomfortably, unsure of how to get rid of us, wondering if we'd ever leave.

M y only constant is the late-night subway. Plodding through the underground tunnels I wait for the train with the Polish cleaning ladies, great statuesque women with broad, flat faces and gold teeth, scarves tied under their chins, ubiquitous Duane Reade drugstore bags between their legs—stolid rows of them calling loudly to each other in Polish. The train arrives and we shuffle in. By the rattling car doors stand clumps of South American busboys with beautiful Aztec faces, laughing with each other in their black pants and white shirts now unbuttoned to reveal gold necklaces gleaming on smooth brown chests. Club kids from the East Village slump against a pole in their consciously ragged outfits, giggling at the conductor as he announces each stop with the unctuous tones of a luxury-car commercial.

Soon it's my stop.

I'm finally home from work.

PROOFREADING

This Stock Purchase Agreement ("Agreement") [As per the regulations of the Securities Exchange Commission] is made as of this 13th day of October, 1989, by and between GRIMM BROTHERS Inc., a London corporation with its principal place of business c/o Hansel & Gretel . . .

Proofreading: Two people sit at a desk. One stares down at the page while the other reads the document aloud by means of a bizarre method of arcane verbal shorthand and physical tics:

This fingertap **Stock** fingertap **Purchase** fingertap **Agreement** "Ag defined brack as per the reggs of the fingertap sex fingertap change fingertap come close brack" **is made as of this** "fig thirteen tee aich day" **thirteenth day of** fingertap **October** "com, fig one nine eight nine" **by and between** handslap **Grimm** handslap **Brothers** handslap "inkpoint com" **a** fingertap **London** fingertap **Corporation with its principal place of business** "cee slash oh" **c/o** . . .

A chance encounter on a street corner with a friend

83

named Cindy led me to this. After a few ad-hoc lessons in coffee shops followed by laborious ten-page tests at temp agencies I was good enough to get work.

My first call sent me to the printer for the Securities and Exchange Commission. "It's usually a long shift," the agency told me. "Fifteen hours or so. Can you do it?"

"Sure."

When I arrive at five P.M. I'm escorted by a guard to a very blond-wood corporate conference room. In the center of the floor is a glass-enclosed space filled with burly working-class guys setting plates to print pages and pages of stock mergers and options. These guys carelessly hold the world of striped ties and millions of dollars in their hands. Standing around, chatting and smoking, are five other people my age waiting for the document to be printed.

I'm assigned to do a full-read with a partner. Menus are sent in at one A.M. We order lobster and steak and coleslaw and french fries. It's like a dinner party. We laugh and pass things around and pour for each other. None of us has eaten like this for a long time. God, I'm thinking to myself, this is fun *and* I'm making eighteen dollars an hour! When I finish at nine A.M. a chauffeured car is waiting downstairs to take me home.

I proofread steadily for five years and never had a night like that again.

To be a proofreader on the midnight shift is to become unstuck in time, divorced from the quotidian rhythm of everyone around you. Waking up from a late-night nap you dress for work as the restaurants buzz. It's midnight when you start work. That's the okay part. Just before dawn is when it's really hard. That's when you're gripped by a gritty, achy feeling and you almost weep at the thought of putting your head down on the desk for just one second. But you don't because a) it isn't allowed and b) you will slide into a dream so fast that when you have to sit up, it is like getting stabbed in the head with a nail.

Leaving work at eight A.M. you have that tired, dirty, after-a-long-plane-ride feeling. Jet lag at a desk. When you step outside, you wince. The day is too loud, the light too bright, the shiny morning passersby seem alien as you walk down the sidewalk, grinning goofily from relief.

When you wake up it's the middle of the day and you're hung over from work. The most normal chores are Herculean labors, you are obsessed only with sleep.

I found full-time work at a white-shoe law firm, where the lawyers at the office were the cream of the crop. They worked hellish hours, but the money was big and there was plenty more where that came from. Their days were filled with easy camaraderie, trading law-school jokes, nicknames for the meanest partners, discussing the rituals of the weekend blowout, the summer rentals in the Hamptons. Sometimes I would sit in a room during a twelve-hour conference, proof-reading a document in the corner, and no one even looked at me. Once, though, when a young lawyer was trying to remember the details of a movie he'd seen, I ventured a word.

"Oh!" I said, looking up. "It's on the stage of the music hall! Oh, I love *The 39 Steps!*"

A chill went through the room, a polite smile flashed, and with it came that horrible frisson of knowing I had just done, in a very small way, the wrong thing. Shame coursed through me and I looked down, pretending to read, absurdly hurt. I felt eight years old.

My shifts were long and quiet, filled with pencils and dictionaries and proofreading partners strumming their fingers. Long, dreary nights with the strange luxury of the chauffeured car like a dollop of *crème fraîche* on a Drake's coffee cake. During this time my route home passed a cemetery. I know, I know, I would say to it every night. I know I'm lucky to be alive. Even when I'm in my airless corporate box sweating over an indecipherable contract.

One night the routine was disrupted and I was sent to the printer's. I was thrilled.

Three A.M. found me hanging out with two young guys, proofreaders from other law firms. We have some downtime on our hands, so we're sitting in the deluxe conference room, drinking sodas, watching a porno channel on the monolithic TV. We're trading temp gossip when suddenly the door bursts open and a yupster lawyer strides in.

"Okay," he says, eyes on the document, "I want this blacklined carefully against the master copy. Make sure you . . ." Hearing the TV he turns to look at the screen and his voice burps in his throat. He sees a gynecologically close shot of a naked writhing woman.

By some unspoken pact none of us acknowledges what's going on and we stare back at him innocently.

"Uh, uh . . . blackline the changes. . . ." he says, now staring fixedly at the table. The TV behind him is emitting moans and wet smacking noises.

"Excuse me?" I ask him a question just to make him look at me. "What about the riders written in pencil?"

"Uh, yes, ignore all changes marked in pencil. . . ."

The porno sounds from the TV are becoming more and more frantic. Our bland faces smile up at him as the sounds crescendo. Stuttering a half-finished sentence he fumbles with the door and hurries out while the three of us sink to the floor, laughing in the silent spasmodic way that hurts the stomach, rolling on our backs and waving our feet in the air.

David, the head proofreader at the law firm, was

really into a power trip. He was balding and combed his hair forward, like statues of the Caesars. If he even smelled that you liked someone, wanted them for a partner, he would never let you read with them. Worse, you had to stop by his desk and tell him when you were going to the bathroom.

For a few weeks in a row—probably because David was busy spiting someone else—I was assigned to read with my friend Jorge, who was tall and good looking and funny and smart. "And in booth number two, Claudia and Jorge." Christ, the joy, the absolute goddamn joy, I would feel at that moment!

On dinner breaks Jorge and I would walk around the corner to Cabana Carioca, where we could buy a takeout dinner for three dollars. We would scuttle back, carrying our both-hands-heavy tin of chicken and rice-and-beans and potatoes, laughing on the street with the shrillness of adolescents at the joy of being outside. Reentering the office was like diving underwater, the same unnatural silence, the same absence of air.

Those Brazilian feasts were our downfall. One night while I was nodding happily to Jorge, my mouth full of rice-and-beans, I looked up and saw David in all his Roman glory standing at the window of our cubicle, glaring down at us.

Three days later I didn't have a job.

By this time, though, I didn't just want another job.

I wanted something to look forward to. I wanted to go to Italy. I wanted to be part of a country that had the quality I wanted: beauty. Not the glossy, skinny kind, but generous and grand. I wanted to be an Italian movie star like Silvana Mangano or Anna Magnani, a glamorous woman from the golden age of Italian film-makers—Fellini, Visconti, Pasolini. A woman who wrapped her hair in chic silk scarves, who wore swoopy sunglasses that hid the eyes and made them unreadable, mysterious.

All I did was work, saving every penny. I worked endless hours in a maze of desks, hunched behind a gray polyester-padded partition while I talked to a friend quietly on the phone and poked straightened paper clips in and out of the wall close to my nose.

One night, as I was going down the elevator, the door opened and a guy got on with me, a low-level guy with a bad tie.

"Hey!" he said. "I hear you're going to Italy!"

"Yes," I said gleefully. "I'm out of here in three more weeks!"

He looked at me then, smiling slightly, and said, "Thirty more years."

LA DOLCE VITA

I landed in Italy, in Milan, and took many, many trains. On the last one, between Terontola and Perugia—a hot, steamy little train with smooth wooden seats—I met two elegant Italian women who bought me an ice cream. I made them laugh by reading the "Introductions" section of my Italian phrase book, which progressed with alarming and hilarious rapidity from "Hi! I'm American and visiting Italy" to "I live alone here. Please be quiet!"

In Perugia my bedroom looked out over red-tiled roofs and my school was a palazzo with Murano glass chandeliers and gold-and-green-painted desks. I giggled on cobbled streets with *gelato al limone* in my mouth and stood in cool, dark churches in front of frescoes of perfect angels in chalky blue robes. Late at night, in my shuttered bedroom, a boy from Siena pulled aside my linen sweater to kiss my sunburned shoulders and I squeezed my eyes shut and clenched my teeth and remembered a moment of despair in Brooklyn when it seemed that I'd blown it. That I would never be young, that nothing would happen, that I would slog through traffic to hide in my apartment and that would be it. Yet here I was. I'd proved myself wrong. I'd proved myself right.

Another train ride, this time from Perugia to Rome, a very different train ride now that I had learned to speak Italian, learned to flirt, learned to be young. I'd come to Rome to complete my transformation. I was now ready to become a movie star. I began perfecting my technique by practicing what I like to call the Art of Speculation:

You're sitting languidly on a chair in the Piazza Navona, in the late afternoon when the sun hits the ochre walls of the city and the light turns the color of honey. You see a man. He is tall, elegant, Italian. He is walking by your table.

"*Scusa* . . ." you say, looking up from under your sunglasses, your voice low, a bit dramatic, suggesting hat and gloves filmed in black and white, ". . . *hai da cendere?*"

"*Certo, bella,*" he says, pulling a box of matches from inside an immaculate suit, a fashionable jacket, a perfectly pressed work shirt.

"*Grazie,*" you say, conscious of him watching your mouth, your mouth in lipstick.

He's bent down slightly, so you must lean toward him, toward the flame. You keep your eyes on the cigarette as you balance your hand by touching his, ever so lightly, with your pinkie finger. Then you look into his face, smile directly, and wait one perfect beat as he shakes out the match and looks right back at you.

"Prego," he murmurs.

A trivial encounter, just a moment when your eyes meet and, in one brief hesitation, the entire tango of the sexes is danced.

Furthering the Art of Speculation, you are sitting in the Piazza Navona. Same place. Same time. You are watching the *passeggiata* (the ritual stroll of the crowds around the square) when a man who is passing your table sees you and stops dead in his tracks. This is not considered aberrant behavior in Italy. Why did he stop? Because you are THERE.

Slowly you turn your head, lowering your glasses slightly. You are nonchalant—which isn't easy, because at this moment the message in his eyes is so blatant, so graphic—*"Oh, cara, ti prendo è ti faccio morire"* (Oh, darling, I'll take you and make you *die)*—that you want to giggle. Well, you're now thinking, I can't resist the tongue slide down the neck, the bending back, back . . .

This is the crucial moment. The moment when you know that to look into his eyes will make you so nervous that your butt muscles will clench. At this moment you must smile a little and look away (your newspaper is a necessity). He will stand there patiently, knowing that you know he's still there, daring you to make eye contact again. Yet you read your paper blindly, holding your breath while you feel that flush in the throat, aware that if you do look up again, things will rapidly progress from speculating to copulating.

He waits a moment, then simultaneously shrugs his shoulders and purses his mouth ruefully and strolls away. You slowly exhale, sip your Campari, and feel exhilarated, daring, and totally in control.

To speak Italian, to play café games, was *meraviglioso,* but it wasn't enough. I wanted to believe that Rome really wanted me. Not just because I'd saved the money for a cheap flight and I could stay with a friend, but because I belonged there.

So I dressed up in a swirly lavender print dress with matching stockings and white lace gloves and bluffed my way past the guards at Cinecittà, the largest movie studio in Rome. Legendary Cinecittà. On the front lawn that day stood a seventy-five-foot papier-mâché elephant in embroidered robes left over from a Fellini movie.

Wandering around the place, trying to look as if I knew where I was going, I spotted a door marked CASTING.

"Go on, now!" I told myself. "Go on!"

I stepped through and confidently introduced myself to one Mr. Cinieri. He was an older man, courteous (he believed my story: a successful young actress here on a whim). He offered me a chair, a drink, a cigarette. But when I told him I wanted work he turned his palms to the ceiling and shook his head.

"Ah," he said sympathetically, "but I want to do something for you. I will call an agent and perhaps . . ."

Squinting through the cigarette smoke he picked up his phone, dialed a number, and rattled off sentences with my name and words like *"New Yorkese . . . simpatica,"* over and over. He hung up the phone and scribbled an address on a piece of paper.

"Go there now."

The agent was a young Spanish woman who screamed on the phone in various languages while simultaneously flipping through pages of magazines that seemed only to be about Princess Caroline of Monaco. She did come through, though, and sent me off to meet with a director making a film about bordellos. Perfect, I thought. A job interview where I didn't have to lie about having the right experience.

I went to meet him the next morning wearing a low-cut black dress, high heels, and tons of makeup. The taxi driver drove the entire way with his eyes fixed to the rearview mirror. I sat in the waiting room, trying not to sweat, desperate for something to drink but not wanting to smear my lipstick. I hoped . . . I don't know what I hoped for, but I couldn't wait for the interview to be over so at the very least I'd have an anecdote for my friends at lunch. An assistant ushered me into the office to meet the director, a squashy, toadlike man with a big cigar. Sitting before him I tried to be as sexy as I could: chest out, eyelashes fluttering. I wanted this job.

He leaned back in his chair and stared at me with pouchy, half-closed eyes.

"Buon giorno," I ventured.

"I speak English," he said, without expression. "Do you sing?"

"Yes!"

"Do you mind wearing a suggestive costume?"

"NO!" I squealed. "I do that every weekend and no one even has a camera!"

"Okay," he responded noncommittally. "We'll let you know."

I returned to New York and waited. Three endless weeks later my phone rang at five-thirty in the morning. It was my agent. I'd gotten the part! I had a real reason to go to Rome. I wasn't just "going to Rome next week." I *had* to go to Rome next week. It was necessary to construct a complex scenario at the law firm where I was proofreading. Illness, bankruptcy, family tragedy—there was no lie I wouldn't tell to have this adventure.

I arrived in Rome the night before my "call" and woke up, predawn, on the sofabed in my friend's apartment. I washed my hair and grabbed a bathrobe

—the only instructions they'd given me—and went downstairs to wait on a Roman street corner in the dark. Eventually, a skinny young guy with greased-back hair and heavy-lidded, sexy eyes pulled up in a tiny Fiat 500. He nodded me in. Shifting and driving, a cigarette dangling in his mouth, he talked nonstop about how getting up this early in the morning ruined his digestion. Several street corners later we picked up a tall Neapolitan girl named Laura. As it turned out, our driver was also Neapolitan and the two of them carried on in unintelligible dialect for the entire trip. I, meanwhile, stared at the bizarre mix of Roman ruins and modern storefronts passing by my window, trying to ignore that first-day-at-a-new-school stomachache.

We drove to the outskirts of Rome and pulled up in front of a small, shabby studio. *Not* Cinecittà. Laura and I joined a group of fifteen young women dressed in their Roman uniforms of miniskirt, big belt, and pumps standing around a guy with a clipboard. He herded us to the dressing rooms, where I discover that mine has my name on it. Because I'm the singer.

I'm so excited, I can barely breathe. I'M A FILM ACTRESS! IN ROME!

"Okay ragazze, spogliatevi è andate direttamente a makeup!" ("Okay girls, take off all your clothes and go to makeup!")

Makeup?! I love makeup. Particularly cakey, heavy

photo makeup. The get-out-the-Silly-Putty-buddy-and-make-me-into-a-grown-woman-without-a-single-expression-line-on-my-face kind of makeup.

I soon found myself in a chair while the makeup artist, an older Italian woman wearing a housecoat and slippers, barely looked at me while she coated my face with thick white foundation. Kabuki white. With eyebrows to match. Next came great swoops of black pencil that went up to my hairline and thick panda rings around my eyes. Beside me sat a girl who was equally pale, only she had red eye shadow and a big black dot in the middle of her forehead. I was starting to feel a little uneasy. The makeup matron turned my now-stricken face toward her and painted my mouth with lipstick the color and texture of tomato paste. She teased my hair into a huge, frizzy mane. This was not at all what I'd had in mind. I'd wanted glamour. Instead I looked like the offspring of a girl from Bensonhurst and a Klingon from *Star Trek*.

Enter the costume designer. He's Swiss. Very gay. Looking us up and down with a pronounced sneer, he commanded us in German-accented Italian to line up outside his door down the hall. I made a silent vow not to be cowed by Swiss Miss. No matter what.

We filed out and lined up, all of us grinning weakly as the first girl went in. We waited, trying not to stare at each other. The door opened and the girl came out. She was wearing a little sailor collar and a little sailor

98

hat. And nothing else. Casually, she shrugged on her bathrobe and walked toward the dressing rooms as the next girl went in.

The door shut.

The door opened.

The girl walked out wearing a drum majorette jacket encrusted with frogs and epaulets. And a change purse. And nothing else. She was visibly more nervous than her predecessor, and held the purse firmly over her crotch. She had a great body.

I want to cry. Oh, my God. This is what the director meant by "suggestive." I'd imagined bare velvet gowns, uplift bras, and *long gloves.* The door opened again and a girl ran giggling to a friend. She was wearing a watch.

I'm next.

Head down, fists clenched, I marched through the door, grabbed the costume designer by both hands, looked into his eyes, and said as sincerely as I've ever said anything in my life: "You have GOT TO GIVE ME SOMETHING TO WEAR!"

This is what he gave me: a sheer black-fringed scarf tied halter-style around my breasts. A thin silver belt with a few wispy-colored chiffon scarves looped on each hip around my waist. Black high heels. Huge yellow plastic earrings. No change purse. Thank God I'd remembered to bring my bathrobe.

The girls separated into two distinct groups. Those

99

of us who wished to die, and a smaller group who thought this was great, a step to stardom—particularly Miss Timex and a small dark girl in vermilion crotchless panties.

The clipboard guy ordered us to the set. Now, I knew that there was a crew, but that hardly mattered. Crews are notoriously indifferent. But while walking with Laura through the dingy studio hallways I hadn't made the leap of logic to understand that in a film about a bordello, there would have to be MEN. This became all too clear as we arrived at a giant curving staircase and at the bottom, staring fixedly up at us, were about thirty of them, a knot of very strange men ranging from a hugely fat bald man to a twisted hunchback with a sad face.

"I can't!" I hissed to Laura. "I *can't!*"

"*Respiri,*" she said firmly, taking my hand. Heads high, we descended the stairs together, striding confidently past the chorus of grinning, catcalling men. "*Buon giorno, bella! Buon giorno, bella!*"

"Eat my shit, ass-wipe!" I smiled back at them with a great big Gidget smile.

The set was a cage of iron bars filled with red velvet poufs. We were herded inside and the door locked behind us. At least, we realized, the men were outside the bars; therefore the scene would not be "interactive." I began to relax, to laugh a bit, to feel I could get through this. How could I quit what I had worked so hard to make possible? How could I go back to my friend's apartment having failed at my adventure?

Here was my role: Stand dead center stage and sing "Them There Eyes." For three solid days. With a smoke machine that smelled vaguely like the incense at High Mass and made my eyes, already irritated from makeup, raw and stinging. In addition I was continually at war with Swiss Miss. Every time he turned away I would yank. the. scarves. forward. Then he would notice and come screaming onto the set ("NO, NO, signorina!") and yank. the. scarves. back. Meanwhile Anita (she of the change purse), who was seated on a pouf to my left, legs tightly crossed, change purse held carefully in her lap, droned on and on with a steady stream of complaints in a nasal Roman accent: "Mamma mia, questa tortura cinese che non finisce mai." Translation: "Oh, mamma, this Chinese torture will never end." Everything she said made me bray with laughter.

Finally, on the last day, during a scene shot sitting down (oh, bliss), she made me laugh so uncontrollably that my elbow hit one of the flats of the set and it fell crashing to the floor.

That night, we all sat around the studio café, drinking out of teeny glass bottles of bitter soda and eating confetti-colored packaged ice cream.

At the last moment, as our cabs pulled up, we started hugging and kissing and crying. This group of young women with pallid, sticky faces and matted hair were suddenly more than friends, more than family. We were leaving behind the only people who would ever understand what we had lived through.

OUTWARD BOUND

The Voice of the World says, "Hey! That's a great story!"

The Voice of the World says, ". . . Um, how old are you now?"

The Voice of the World says, "It's time to stop having 'stories,' Claudia. It's time to have a life."

I brush this aside with a smile and a wave while inside I moan, They're right. They're right. I'm fucked. I'm gonna end up a supermarket checkout clerk holding up a giant roll of toilet paper, screaming, "Herbie, is there a rain check on the ScotTissue?"

No. No. I still believe in adventure. I still believe what I read. I still believe in getting out of the house.

When my friend's parents sent her a thrilling brochure for a Hurricane Island Outward Bound course, I grabbed it. Colorful, bold-type letters on the front page threw down the gauntlet: CAN YOU DO IT?

Yesss!

With the help of a Reader's Digest Scholarship, a pair of $1.99 baby-blue sneakers from ABC Bargain Stores on Graham Avenue in Greenpoint, Brooklyn,

103

and a ratty Basque beret for a bit of panache, I rode the bus from Port Authority Bus Terminal in New York for eleven hours up to a tiny bus stop in Rockland, Maine. I was ready to be hearty. I was ready to be salty. I had learned sea chanties and read books about trials in the wilderness. I was ready for my twenty-eight-day sea course.

Twenty-eight days of pure quaking terror.

I arrived in a daze of bus-trip exhaustion and stood on the dock with my duffel among a jumble of clueless students being shepherded onto a large boat by jovial, tanned Olympians. These were our "watch officers," or "watch-o's" as they called themselves. The first thing they did was divide us into "watches" of twelve, with two "watch-o's" per group. My watch consisted of four girls and eight gangly seventeen-year-old boys. We were each assigned a number, *"a number that could save your life in a sea emergency!"*

The next morning, disoriented and cramped from sleeping in a tent, I was awakened at five A.M. by a bright Olympian voice. "Okay! Run and dip!" Run and dip?

"What is run and dip?" I croaked.

"Well," said the voice, "we run two and a half miles on the beach and then we go for a dip in the ocean."

"But it's raining!" I bleated.

Roars of laughter from the watch-o's.

Skidding, falling, panting, plodding, I made my

way around what I considered a very poorly constructed island. There were huge gaps between boulders that I insisted on traversing by sliding on my haunches instead of attempting the ludicrous leaps I was encouraged to try. Then, after retching violently at the finish line, I was put on the end of a straggly, shivery line of students and told to JUMP INTO THE OCEAN. IN MAINE. AT APPROXIMATELY SIX A.M.

Looking down from the edge of the dock, down fifteen feet at the icy gray water, freezing in my bathing suit, pale and goose-pimply, I suddenly realized this was what the course would be. I had no place in this adventure. I was so ashamed, so afraid.

"I can't," I whimpered, "I can't. I'll have a heart attack and die."

"Just do it!" a big guy with a funny accent said kindly. "Everyone does. It's great!"

Now I'm reduced to begging and weeping.

"Well," he said, "if you don't go in soon, your group will miss breakfast. And it's *pancakes*."

I'm immediately surrounded by a rabid pack of seventeen-year-old boys chanting, "Jump! Jump! Please, please jump!" They are almost in tears too. If I didn't jump soon I knew I would have to leave the course, disgraced. Sidling up to edge of the dock I look down again. I want to go, I really do, but my body won't move.

105

"Push me!" I say, gritting my teeth. "Someone push me!"

"I'll push her! I'll push her!" Many voices.

"No," orders the big guy. "She has to do it herself."

So I screwed my eyes shut and, with an unearthly wail, stepped out into nothingness. The feeling of falling was horrible and the shock of the cold, cold water popped my eyes open as I desperately swam for the float, teeth clacking, involuntary little "Ungh unghs" rattling in my throat.

The days passed with me begging, crying, nose clogged with snot, dripping sweat, falling, scraping my hands, my knees, my face, my ass. I was fat, pasty, I had no cool outdoor clothing (the wilderness has a fashion code as rigid as the chicest neighborhood in New York), I was without ego, without past. I was lost in an alien land. There was no parallel in my life.

Nothing about growing up in Brooklyn had prepared me for the primal, all-enveloping fear of being a speck on an endless wall of granite, empty space all around me, clinging desperately to the rock face, one toe braced on an M & M–size knob, one hand wedged in a crack the width of a dime, the other hand scrabbling for something, *anything,* to hold on to. I had wanted to be like a hero in the wilderness—the clean line of the jaw clenched stoically through moments of adversity—"To be afeard of a thing and yet to do it is what makes the prettiest kind of a man." Instead I

106

found myself muttering in the utterly unselfconscious way insane people do: *Oh God okay okay I'm gonna move my foot oh jeez okay oh please move the foot okay moving the foot.*

Our first sailing expedition: open boat, thirty feet long, twelve of us crammed in, stupefied, staring out at the ocean, thankful to sit down, thinking about lunch.

The sails are up and we're slapping along when a guy named Mateus climbs over to Paul, the instructor. Paul is the big guy with the accent, a huge French Canadian with a bushy brown beard and bright, crinkly eyes.

"Uh, Paul? Uh, uh"—his voice lowered—"where do we go to the bathroom?"

"Anywhere you like!" said Paul, waving his arm over the ocean. "Anywhere you like!"

OHMYGOD. Climbing granite cliffs is a breeze compared to this. At least you get to keep your pants on. But to make a doody in front of a dozen people! I couldn't bring myself to pee. And I held it in, too, for quite a few hours, until I had reached a point where I didn't care if they flew in a camera crew and made a documentary. Bare butt over the side of the boat, one hand gripping the wire shroud, the other braced on the gunwale, I tried desperately to relax, relax, to do it as quickly as possible, biting down a scream as a frigid wave smacked my bottom.

I wasn't alone, though. One young girl, a Mexican millionairess named Maru Ruiz Francia, was perfectly willing to die of toxic shock rather than "go" in this fashion. So in the grand tradition of Outward Bound teamwork, all the girls would go to the bow and hold up their towels to form a partition. Then Maru would delicately lower her pants, cross herself, and heave her hips onto the gunwale. My job was to help *her* relax. I did this by standing next to her and singing, "If ever I would leave you, it wouldn't be in springtime . . ." And off in the stern we would hear Paul laugh and laugh and laugh.

Paul was great. He was the real thing. I didn't have a crush on Paul. I worshiped him. He was my hero, a hero like in my books, like in my dreams. He laughed at everything; not a snide, commenting kind of laugh, but a hearty, joyful guffaw. "Hey! Go ahead! Go on, now! It make you happy, hokay?" And when I finished the climb, the run, the scary jump, he'd be waiting for me, beaming and laughing. "Hokay, you happy now?" And looking into his merry face, I'd have to laugh with him.

One night, at two A.M., the instructors woke us. This time we had to work our way in the pitch dark through an impossibly small crack in an immense half-mile-long boulder. Silent, except for grunts of effort, we clutched each other's sleeves as we inched forward, wriggling our bodies against the pebbly sur-

108

face of the granite. Midway, rock around me, under me, pressing my back, my face, suffocating, unable to move, I lost it. My breath began to wheeze out of me in a keening note of panic, but then, way above me, looking down from the top of the boulder, his face eerily lit by a miner's lamp, was Paul. Laughing.

"Hey! What is dat racket? You gonna wake up de whole island! C'mon, now! You gonna do it! It make you happy, hey?"

I did it.

Sooner or later Paul got me to do everything. From the top of a climbing cliff he would urge me on, his helmet pushed to a rakish angle, legs dangling over the edge.

"C'mon! C'mon up! Dere to your right is something. . . . Oh! It's as big as me! Step on dat!"

Meanwhile I was dying, my face jammed in some rock crevice.

"Shut up, Paul! Fuck you!"

"Oh, Claudee! I can hear you!"

Paul walked like a big cat. He would pick things off trees and eat them. He could build a fire and sail and climb and run. He was brave. He'd had real adventures. He could pick me up.

During a late-night sail, when the whole world was just ocean and stars and everyone had pulled into their foul weather gear like turtles, he stood against the mast, perfectly balanced, perfectly at ease, with me

109

huddled at his feet. We sang together. *"Vous avez nom que je voudrais pour ma maîtresse, vous avez nom que les amours voudraient connaître."* Singing up at him my heart felt like a balloon.

Toward the end of the course my watch was taken to a large pond. Our mandate was to build a raft from scattered bits of old buoys and sail rope, then float across to the opposite bank. This we did, messy and makeshift and in our underwear. After twenty-five days we had learned the great lessons of the wilderness: 1) Keep whatever you can dry, 2) eat anything you're offered, 3) hide toilet paper somewhere on your person.

Finishing our "group task" we sat down in a circle to "talk about it"—who helped the most, who took the initiative, who didn't, et cetera. "Hokay," said Paul. "Let's say you are going on an expedition. A real one. Now each person choose a crew."

Around the joking, cheering group we went, everyone choosing their ten team members. I kept smiling, fixedly, as each person made a list of names that didn't include me.

"Well," said Paul, "now it's my turn. If I were going on an expedition, I would choose Claudia."

Claudia?! ME?!

"Yes," said Paul, his face serious, "because in de wilderness, when tings get tough, who runs de fastest

110

or does tings best doesn't matter. It's a sense of humor, a sense of humor. And Claudia, she has dat."

Rarely does someone show you a portrait of yourself—clean, clear, and totally unexpected. Never mind the sword pulling from the stone, *this* is the adventure. If, for a moment, you see someone differently, their portrait changes.

It comes to life.

PINK DOUGHNUT

I'm standing on line at one of those doughnut places in New York's Penn Station, marking time, waiting for a train, wanting an iced coffee. In front of me is a guy—tall, fair, handsome, so I notice him. He's carrying a Lands' End bag with that tennis-racket pocket thing. I'm perusing the doughnuts, watching him out of the corner of my eye, amused because I love watching grown-ups order treats, hearing men's deep voices saying things like "Uh, no, I want the pink one with the sprinkles, please." I look up as he suddenly throws money on the counter, half the small change bouncing to the floor. The small Hispanic woman who has been helping him flinches, and that does it for me. That flinch. That blink of fear, the twist of the mouth that is the insult finding its mark.

"Why did you do that?" I can't help myself.

"Do you know how much they charge for coffee and a doughnut here?"

"So? She works here, for godsake! She works here in *Penn Station*! She probably works for minimum wage under the horrible lights of Penn Station and

113

you're catching a train to go away for the weekend with a tennis racket and you're *throwing* money at her?"

"Uh, it's really expensive." He turns his back to me and starts to walk away.

"You overprivileged fat-assed white motherfucker!"

Back he turns. "I don't appreciate your attitude." The muscles in his cheek are twitching.

Quietly, my teeth clicking, I say, "Have you no shame? Have you no perspective?"

He walks away and I'm left, as always, with the adrenaline like pus in my stomach while the people in the place glance at me, then look furtively away. But the woman behind the counter looks directly at me.

"Thanks," she mouths silently.

Leaving, I pass by a table filled with Puerto Rican drug dealers and the white women who love them.

"C'mere!" They call me over. "C'mere. C'mere!"

"What?"

"Hey. Hey, good for you!"

Good for me? Well, this is what I think: You talk to people who serve you the food the same way you talk to the people you eat the food with. You talk to people who work for you the same way you talk to the people you work for. It's a one-size-fits-all proposition. Talk to people. People will show you classical Indian dance, karate katas, equine dressage; explain Hegel, Jung, Iris Murdoch, Prince; tell you about their hometown in Colombia, Sicily, Tasmania, Moscow. And make you laugh.

Once I was waitering in a ritzy restaurant in Chelsea. Those of us on the late shift were starving, so when we spied a busboy heading to the kitchen with an untouched steak we took off. He was a Peruvian Pied Piper and four of us fell in behind him, pushing and shoving and tearing at the steak with our hands. Suddenly the door to the kitchen swung open and we all froze, guilty, afraid it was the manager. But it was just another waiter who said, without missing a beat, "Oh, look! *Dances With Wolves!*"

Sitting on rooftops, desktops, countertops, under counters; perched on milk crates, wine crates, paper cartons, front steps; hanging out in back alleys, deserted cafeterias, spooky hallways, we are all the same: a motley crew of artsy-fartsy types and single mothers and social misfits and immigrants who work six days, double shifts and send all the money home. We are people in recovery, people in denial, gay guys shocking the shit out of pizza guys from Queens—and vice versa. We all fit in because none of us belongs anywhere. And, boy, what you can learn: dirty words in every language and the fact that nobody is just a typist, just a dishwasher, just a cook, just a porter, just a prostitute. That everyone has a story. Everyone has at least one story that will stop your heart.

115

Is this disjointed? I don't think so. Life doesn't have a topic sentence. There is nothing as clichéd as a story of a road traveled, of lessons learned, of obstacles overcome. But that's because it's the only story, the *big* story, simple as reading something in a book as a child. Something that sounds made up, like the phases of the moon. Then one night you look at the sky and realize that it's true, that you can see it for yourself.

And that's all I can say, really. These things are true and I've seen them for myself.